HEROES
AND
OUTLAWS

OF THE BIBLE

Downhome Reflections of History's
Most Colorful Men and Women

DON REID

foreword by JIMMY DEAN

New Leaf Press

First printing: June 2002
Second printing: August 2004

ISBN: 0-89221-526-7
Library of Congress Catalog Card Number: 2002105544

Printed in the United States of America.

Please visit our website for other great titles:
www.newleafpress.net

For information regarding author interviews, please contact the publicity department at (870) 438-5288.

To Jack,

who taught me how

ACKNOWLEDGMENTS

It takes a lot of people to write a book. If you think I did this all by myself, thanks for the confidence, but here's a few of the good folks who helped.

At New Leaf Press: Roger Howerton, my first contact and first friendly voice in the publishing business; Brent Spurlock, the art director who coordinated the cover of the book (something I hope the text lives up to); Jim Fletcher, the editor who gave me a wide and tree-swinging swath; Laura Welch, a sweet and gentle publicist (and up to now I thought that was an oxymoron); and Tim Dudley, the president, who brought it all together with a quiet and gentlemanly air.

On my end: Russ Farrar, my friend and agent and attorney who went those extra steps to make it all work; Jimmy Dean, my pal with a heart the size of his home state; Joe Brandon, my minister who helped me pronounce the biblical names for the audio book (try King Ahasuerus on for size sometime); Debo and Langdon, my sons and sounding boards who proofed and encouraged and helped me record; and Debbie, my sweet wife who endured long nights and days of me at the computer and always told me how good it was even if it wasn't.

Bless you all.

CONTENTS

Foreword 7

Preface 9

Abraham 13

Joseph 39

Gideon 67

Samson 83

Ruth 101

Elijah 113

Esther 135

John the Baptist 153

FOREWORD

Don Reid has been a friend of mine for a long, long time and I am indeed proud to call him friend. He is not only a friend of mine, but I am a fan of his. I love his singing; he is a fine composer and has one of the greatest comedic minds I have ever run into.

But just when I think that I know about all there is to know about Don Reid, he will do something that will surprise and amaze me, as it is with this book, *Heroes and Outlaws of the Bible.*

I have known all along that Don is a very religious and spiritual person, but until I read this book I was unaware that he was such a well-versed biblical student. And that great knowledge is certainly evident in *Heroes and Outlaws of the Bible.*

I must say that knowing Don personally has certainly enabled me to enjoy this writing more. Though Don is a serious person, I have learned that underneath all that ability and talent lies his wonderful, wry sense of humor. So many times during the reading of this book I could see, hear, and feel that marvelous sense of humor creeping in. And on more than one occasion something would simply crack me up because I could see Don with that wry grin spread across his face. As you read this book, you will be able to ascertain in many places what I am talking about. I am sure that you will note some of the phraseology is not totally biblical.

I can truthfully say that having read this book I am better informed about several things. I know a little more about the Bible; a little more about the amazing Don Reid; a little bit more about the world we live in; and a little bit more about myself.

Jimmy Dean

PREFACE

I have always been a big movie fan. I went to the movies every Saturday morning without fail when I was a kid growing up in Staunton, Virginia, in the beautiful Shenandoah Valley. Some kids went fishing and camping on the weekends, but not me. It was the old Strand Theater without fail. This was in the fifties, and my favorites were the cowboys, Roy and Gene, of course, Martin and Lewis, the Bowery Boys, and just about anything that moved and you could eat popcorn to.

It was 1955 and I was ten years old, and my friend Bobby and I went around the corner one Saturday morning to the Dixie Theater, which had the reputation of showing more adult movies. In those days "adult movies" meant just that. Something kids would probably not be interested in. *A Man Called Peter* was playing and for some reason or another we went in.

Now, *A Man Called Peter* was the story of a Scotsman, Peter Marshall, who became a Presbyterian preacher and eventually the chaplain for the United States Senate. It was a wonderful movie and it stuck with both of us for years. A short way into the movie there is a scene where a young Peter Marshall trips and nearly falls into a hole or off a cliff or some such similar fate. This is the moment of his conversion. The instant of the reality that Christ was taking hold of his life. Fate at its most dramatic second. And I loved it and relived it in my mind many, many times. The only problem was I never had one of those moments myself. I always wanted one. I was always looking for one and hoping that it was just around the corner, but it never came. Never that defining moment of being hit over the head with the realization that this is what God wants me to remember as that special moment.

My earliest recollections are of going to church. My mother took us as babes in arms. There was no nursery then, so I was there right in the middle of the morning worship service every Sunday. I went to Sunday school from the time I could walk and got perfect attendance pins. I got those little papers that had a color picture on one side and a Bible story on the other. I got a Bible for my eighth birthday from Aunt Ethel and I carried it and read it until the cover began to fall off and the pages fall out. I still have it. It's laying on my desk, not three feet away, at this very moment. It's full of memories and so am I.

I have always known Jesus, thanks to my mother. She took us all — my brother and my sister and myself — to church and we absorbed and learned without even knowing it. And I think the most important thing she gave us and instilled in us was the "habit." The habit of being at church on Sunday morning. None of us has lost that "habit."

My life's work has required me to travel and tour the world and be gone sometimes two weekends out of the month. But on those weekends I was at home, I never failed to attend church. I'm a long-standing elder in the same Presbyterian church I grew up in. I've been a member since I was 12 years old and I don't expect to ever go anywhere else. Oh, I often go on the road and visit other denominations and it's been a blessing. But I'm usually looking at my watch and imagining what is going on at my home church back in Virginia.

I have passed on the same "habit" to my two sons, Debo and Langdon. They, too, are elders in the same church and one of them shares Sunday school teaching duties with me on the Sundays when I'm traveling. My wife, Deborah, is also a Sunday school teacher at the neighboring Baptist church. We might differ a little on "sprinkling" and "dunking" and the merits of Disneyland, but we serve the same God.

So I have never had that emotional conversion story to tell. But my way has been just as sweet. Whether I was sitting in the pew beside my mother (she and I still sit in that same pew today and she's 90 years old and never misses a Sunday) or whether I was serving communion with my sons or teaching Sunday school, I have always felt a sincere closeness to God. I believe in the salvation of Jesus Christ and I pray daily for those who don't know Him.

I never had to seek Jesus. He was always there. He always knew exactly where I was even during times when I didn't. I learned many years ago that it's a gift. You don't work for it or earn it. You don't deserve it or keep a scorecard. You just let it happen and enjoy it. And thank God, I'm enjoying it.

ABRAHAM

Genesis 11–25

Abraham is known to all of us as "The Father of the Faithful." So what is he doing in a book with outlaws in the title? Hey, nobody's perfect, which makes him the perfect example for every one of us. He had his little weaknesses, which God used to make him a stronger man, and to make him the perfect subject to begin this look at good human beings who did saintly and sinful things, all to the final glory of God.

Born Abram, son of Terah about 300 years after the Flood, he grew up in the land of Ur and married a beautiful woman named Sarai. Along with Sarai, his father, and his nephew, Lot, Abram moved up the road to Haran. And it was here that God spoke to him and started him on a life's journey that would set the tone for all our religious heritage.

God said to Abram, "Get up and get out of this country. I'll show you where to go. I'll make you into a great nation. I'll make your name great. I'll bless you and I'll curse whoever stands against you."

And Abram did exactly as he was told. This is a pretty

strong faith. He took his wife and his nephew (his father had died by then), all his possessions, his slaves, his live- stock, and moved to Canaan. If this obedience to God sounds impressive at this point, let me add one more thing that makes it even more difficult to grasp. Abram was not a young man. At this point in his life, when God spoke to him and when he uprooted his entire family and estate, he was 75 years old. And this is where the story is just beginning.

Abram moved around in Canaan and built altars in dif- ferent regions and was promised by God that his descendants would one day own the land he was living on. But the land would not always be the most desirable, and this was proven by a famine that set in and forced Abram to head down to Egypt to live until the hard times passed. Crossing borders into a foreign country was not always a safe prospect, and just before he entered Egypt with his wife, he stopped and thought it through and said to her, "Sarai, you're a beautiful woman. And when those Egyptians see you, they're going to kill me to get to you. So here's what we need to do. Let's tell everybody over there that you're my sister and that way they won't feel a need to kill me in order to get to you."

Now Sarai must have been one lovely woman to have stirred those kinds of emotions in men. To admire a woman's beauty is one thing; to kill for it is another. But Abram turned out to be right. They did want her and that little lie did save Abram's life. But there's one thing we need to get straight before we go any further. That "little lie" was only half a lie. Sarai was Abram's wife but she was also his half-sister. I won't try to justify this. I'm only reporting the facts. The only thing it justifies is that Abram was not a total liar.

Just as he expected, when they got to Egypt, the men couldn't keep their eyes off his wife. She must have been a striking woman, considering she was no longer a flower of youth. To take the Scriptures literally, she was only ten years younger than Abram, which would make her 65 years old. And when the pharaoh's men saw this mature, lovely, woman, they showered her with attention and praise and showed her to Pharaoh and she was immediately taken into Pharaoh's palace and we must assume into his harem.

Pharaoh liked what he saw and in return showered her "brother" with gifts. He gave Abram sheep and cattle and donkeys and camels and servants.

But God didn't like what he saw. He inflicted Pharaoh and all his family with plagues. His entire household came down with terrible diseases, all because of this Jewish woman who had come to live there. And the pharaoh seemed to understand why it was all happening because he called Abram in and said, "What have you done to me? Why did you tell me this woman was your sister?"

"Well, actually she really is my —"

"Why didn't you tell me she was your wife?"

"Well, yeah, I guess she is my —"

"Do you know how much trouble you've caused around here?"

"Well, I guess I have but —"

"Abram, take this woman and get out of here. Keep all that stuff I gave you, all the livestock and servants. You can have it all but just get her and get on your way and out of my sight."

So Abram left Egypt an even wealthier man. Besides his newly acquired livestock, he was dealing in silver and gold. He moved around some more, as he could well afford to, and wound up near a place called Bethel. His nephew Lot was with him and they became business partners. Lot's wealth also grew and he and Abram owned so much stuff between the two of them that their employees began arguing and fighting one another. They had outgrown the land and they were crowding each other.

Abram came to his nephew and said, "Let's not fall out. I'd rather we split up than wind up mad at each other. So let's do this. You take all your people and go in the direction you choose. I'll go in the opposite direction."

And this is exactly what they did. Lot went east toward Sodom and pitched his tents and became a city boy while Abram stayed out in the country near Hebron.

After Lot left, God came to Abram and said, "Look north, south, east, and west. For as far as you can see, I'll give this land to your children and your children's children and to all your generations. You will have so many offspring you won't be able to count them."

He didn't say anything at the time, but this promise must have struck Abram as somewhat odd, as he was now seventy-five years old and still didn't have even one child much less more than he could count.

Kings and nations fell out with kings and nations and as always in history there were battles and wars and the shedding of blood. The cities of Sodom and Gomorrah were taken and Lot, Abram's nephew, who was living near Sodom, was kidnapped along with all his family. All his possessions were taken, but one of his people, who managed to escape, found his way to Abram's camp and told "Abram the Hebrew" what had happened.

Now you might find it interesting that this is the first time the word "Hebrew" is used in the Bible. The word originally did not mean what it later came to mean. In Egypt, when they referred to Hebrews, they were talking about the nomads, the wanderers, the migrant workers. As it so happened, more times than not, those nomads and wanderers and migrant workers were the Israelites, the Jewish people. Thus, Hebrew became synonymous with Israelite. And when the Scriptures refer to "Abram the Hebrew" they're not talking about that stalwart pillar of Jewish ancestry. They're talking about that nomad who moved around in the desert all the time from Ur to Haran to Shechem to Negev to Bethel to Hebron.

And by the time the escapee from Lot's camp found him, Abram was living in Mamre. When he heard what had happened to his old partner and son of his brother, he gathered up 318 well-trained men and went off into the night to bring him back. Now this Abram is a little different creature from the one who cowered down in Egypt in the face of danger and let his wife be taken into the pharaoh's harem to save his own hide. This was an angry warrior in pursuit of justice and his mission was successful. He brought Lot and all his possessions back safely and in one piece.

The kings of Sodom and of Salem came out to meet the triumphant Abram and to sing his praises. Melchizedek, the king of Salem, brought him bread and wine and said to him, "Blessed be God for He has delivered your enemies to you." And Abram was touched and gave Melchizedek a tenth of all he had recovered in the battle.

But when the king of Sodom said to him, "You can keep all those spoils of war for yourself, just give me my people back," Abram bristled. He didn't like this king or anything he stood for. He didn't like the things he had heard that went on in his city and he didn't approve of Lot living up there amid all that mess. He had rallied the troops because Lot was blood kin, but he didn't have to like it.

Abram looked the king in the eye and said, "I don't want to be indebted to you in any way. No favors. No deals. I wouldn't take a thread from your sandal. I would never want you to be able to say, 'I made Abram rich.' "

Abram was showing an edge we haven't seen before. But this was just the beginning of the changes this man called Abram was about to feel.

God came and talked to Abram again. Abram was apparently suffering from letdown-after-the-victory syndrome. He was in the dumps and God reassured him and told him not to be afraid.

"But I have no children, God," Abram blurted out. "Nobody to work for and live for. No one to inherit my fortunes. I'll wind up leaving everything I have to Eliezer, a servant in my house."

"No," God said. "This servant will not be your heir. You'll have a son. Look up at the heavens. Can you count all those stars? That's how many heirs you'll have. You are going to be the father of generations."

"God, You also told me I would have all the land I could see in any direction. How do I know that's going to happen?"

This Abram, strong of faith, was not showing much strength at this time. He had so little faith in what God had told him about the children he would father, that he had since made out his will in favor of a servant in his house. He had so little faith in the promise of land God had made him that he was now asking for some proof; some hope. Sounds like just another struggling soul trying to figure out life, doesn't it?

At this point God instructs Abram in a rather bizarre ritual. He has him fetch a three-year-old heifer, goat, and ram, along with a dove and a pigeon. He has him slice the heifer, goat, and ram in two, and as night falls Abram falls into a deep trance. During this trance God tells him his descendants will be slaves in a foreign country for four hundred years but that they will be rescued and will flourish. He then assures him he will live until a good old age and die peacefully.

Then in the night, a blazing torch appeared from nowhere and passed between the sliced pieces of the heifer and the goat and the ram. And this was God's way of signing a deal, sealing a covenant, ratifying a pact, securing an agreement. Now Abram could be sure that for as far as he could see, his descendants for as far as he could count, would be living under the caring and watchful eye of God.

ABRAHAM II

Sarai, Abram's wife, was getting more restless as her biological clock ticked away. She was sure she would never have any children and she so wanted Abram to have sons and daughters that she went to him and said, "Honey, I don't think it's going to happen for us. So why don't you sleep with my girl servant, Hagar. She can have your babies and you can build a family through her. I know she's Egyptian, but it's better than having no sons at all."

Now this arrangement was not as unusual then as it would be today, so we have to give Abram a *little* slack at jumping at the offer. We may want to question *faithful* old Abram for again not trusting God to do it the way He had promised, but maybe he thought this was God's way of doing it. Maybe he thought he was doing the right thing, doing the will of God. Or maybe he was a little bit excited at sleeping with the young Hagar. Whatever the answer,

Abram's answer to Sarai's proposal was, "Okay!"

But when Hagar, the maid, first realized she was pregnant, things changed quickly and bitterly. She started to strut around in front of Sarai, the wife, and give off an attitude that only one spiteful woman can give another. She began to despise Sarai.

Sarai went to Abram and said, "Look at what you've done. You're responsible for every bit of this. Look at how my maid treats me now. Just what are you going to do about this mess you've caused?"

So here was poor ole Abram, caught between two feuding women, wishing it were only the devil and the deep blue sea. He had done what his wife told him to do and now he was being blamed for it. He took the only defense he could. "She's your maid, Sarai. You handle it. It was your idea. Leave me out of it."

And Sarai did, gladly. She began to treat Hagar like dirt beneath her feet and took pride in lording over her as mistress over a servant. And Hagar, confused and bested, ran. She took off out through the desert with no particular place in mind. To get away from Sarai was her only destination.

An angel found her by a spring along the road out in the wilderness. And he said to her, "Hagar, where'd you come from and where're you going?"

"I'm running away from Sarai."

"Don't," the angel said. "Go back to her and brace up and take your medicine. Do all of this and I promise you your descendants will be more than you can count. The baby you're carrying now will be a son. Call him Ishmael. That means 'God hears' because God has heard about the troubles you're having.

"Now this son, Ishmael, will be a wild man. He'll be

against everybody and everybody will be against him. Belligerent. Warlike. That will be his nature. But I urge you to go back and have this baby and live with Abram and Sarai."

And Hagar did as the angel of the Lord told her to do and she bore Abram a son and they named him Ishmael. And when his first son was born, Abram was 86 years old.

God appeared and talked to Abram again. This time it was 13 years after Ishmael's birth. But the message was pretty much the same as it had always been. He was assuring Abram again of all the offspring he would have. He started off by saying, "You will no longer be called Abram [which means 'exalted father']. You will, from now on, be called Abraham [which means 'father of many'] because, as I've told you before, I am going to make you the father of many, many nations. But first I want to establish a covenant with you."

Now God had already told all of this to Abraham before and had already established a covenant with him. Remember the cow, the goat, the ram, and the flaming torch? But it seems that God had done all the giving and all the showing, and what he wanted from Abraham was some sort of commitment from his side. We know that a deal is only as good as the faith of both parties. And this was what God was looking for, some good faith from Abraham.

"Abraham, here is what I want from you. I want you to be circumcised. And I want you to circumcise every male in your family and household for all generations to come. Whether they are your blood or your slaves and servants, I want them circumcised eight days after they're born. Anyone who is not will be cut off from his people. This is very important. This is a covenant of the flesh and is everlasting. This shows me your commitment and sincerity and I, in return, will show you my commitment and sincerity."

God continued, "As for Sarai, her name will now be Sarah" (which means "princess"). "She will give you a son and she will be known as the mother of nations and kings will come from her."

Abraham fell down on the ground on his face and did a strange thing in the presence of God. He laughed. He said to himself, *I'm 99 years old. And God is telling me I'm going to have a son when I'm 100 years old and my wife is 90?*

And here that old *faithfulness* showed up again. God told him what was going to happen and he laughed in His face.

"God," Abraham said, "Can't you just bless Ishmael? He's already my son. Won't that work?"

"Your wife, Sarah, will bear you a son by this time next year. And you will call him Isaac. He is the one I will establish and continue my covenant with. As for Ishmael, I'll bless him. I'll make him a ruler and the father of 12 kings and the head of a great nation. Don't worry about Ishmael."

And then God left and on that very day Abraham gathered Ishmael and his entire male household and circumcised them. Abraham was 99 when he was circumcised and Ishmael was 13.

The Lord came again to Abraham at Mamre, but this time in human form. Abraham, sitting outside his tent in the heat of the day, looked up and saw three men standing nearby. He got up and went to greet them and showed great hospitality. "Sit down in the shade, gentlemen, and let me get you some water to wash your feet. Also, I'll get you something to eat before you continue on your journey."

"That would be very nice if you would," the three men said.

So Abraham ran back into the tent and told Sarah, "Get some flour ready and bake some bread." And then he went out back to the herd and cut out a young calf and gave it to one of the servants to kill and dress. He gathered up butter and milk and served the three men a hearty meal under the shade tree. He was an attentive and gracious host.

"Where is Sarah?" the men asked.

"She's in the tent."

One of the men spoke, the one who was the Lord, and said, "I'll return to you again about this time next year and then Sarah, your wife, will have a son."

He was standing with his back to the tent when he said this and Sarah was standing inside, out of sight. When she heard what he had said she laughed to herself, *I'm an old worn-out woman and my husband is ten years older than I am. He thinks I'm going to have a child at my age?*

Sarah was a little amused and more than a little skeptical of all this talk of her pending motherhood. But these feelings soon turned to fear when she heard the God/man outside her tent say to Abraham, "Why did Sarah laugh? Is anything too hard for the Lord? I'll tell you one more time. When I come back here next year, Sarah will have a son." The Lord had spoken.

With fear trembling in her voice, Sarah called from inside the tent, "I didn't laugh. I didn't laugh."

Without turning around, the Lord said, "Yes, you did laugh."

The three prepared to leave and turned down the road toward Sodom. Abraham, ever the good host, walked a ways with them. They stopped and the one who was the Lord said, "Abraham, you will become the head of a great and powerful nation and all the nations on earth will be blessed through you, so I won't hide from you what I am about to do. The outcry against the cities of Sodom and Gomorrah and their sinful ways is so great that I'm going down there to see if they are really as bad as everyone is saying they are."

The other two men/angels turned and walked toward Sodom and Gomorrah, but the Lord remained standing there with Abraham.

"If you find sin and wickedness, as we have all heard about, will you destroy the entire cities? Will you wipe out the wicked with the righteous? The good with the bad? Certainly you won't do something as horrible as that will you? You won't treat the good people the same way you treat the bad ones will you?"

Abraham was getting brazen questioning the Lord this way. But the one thing that motivated him to talk to God in this manner was the fact that his nephew Lot still lived in Sodom and he was doing all he could to see that Lot wouldn't be unjustly harmed.

"What if there're 50 righteous people there? Will you spare the city if there're 50 righteous people?" Abraham asked.

"If I find 50 righteous people in the city of Sodom, I'll spare the city," God assured him.

"Lord, I know I'm only dust and ashes and I know I'm being way too bold, but what if you only find 45 righteous people? What then?"

"If I find 45, I'll spare it."

"What if you only find 40?"

"If there's 40, I won't destroy the city."

"Now, Lord, don't get mad at me, but let me ask you, if there's only 30, what will you do?"

"If there's 30, Abraham, I'll not do anything."

"Now I don't want to push this thing too far, Lord, and I don't want you to think hard of me, but let me just ask this. What if you only find 20 good people? What then?"

"For the sake of 20 good people, I'll not destroy the city."

"Okay, God, I know I'm probably taking this too far, but I just have to ask. What about 10?"

"Abraham, if there are 10 good people in the city, it will stand."

And then the Lord left and Abraham, having argued with God, turned and went home.

ABRAHAM III

The two angels who turned toward Sodom arrived there in the evening and what happened that night is really Lot's story. But because Abraham bargained with God on behalf of his nephew and begged for considerations on destroying the city, it needs to be told under the banner of Abraham.

The two angels found Lot sitting at the city gates. He was apparently an important city father because this is where important city fathers usually sat.

As soon as he saw them coming, he got up and bowed down to the ground and invited them to his house. He said, "Please come over to my house. I'll give you a place where you can wash up and spend the night."

Being a polite and generous host must have run in the family because Lot treated them almost the same way Abraham had. But they refused Lot.

"No thank you. We'll just sleep out here on the street."

"No, no. I insist," said Lot. "Come to my house and I'll fix you something to eat. I'll bake some bread and then you can go to sleep and get up early in the morning and be on your way to wherever you're going."

So they did. They went with him, ate supper, and just

as they were about to go to bed they heard a commotion outside. They looked out and all the men of Sodom, young and old, had surrounded the house. They yelled in to Lot, "Where are those two men we saw you take inside tonight? Bring them out here so we can have sex with them."

Lot squeezed out the door and closed it tightly behind him and said, "Please don't do this. This is a wicked thing you want to do."

Lot was protecting his guests and he proceeded to protect them at any cost, because the next thing he said showed he had gone over the top at being a good host. "Look, I have two daughters who are virgins. Neither one has ever slept with a man. I'll bring them both out here and you all can do whatever you want to do. Have your way with them however you want, but don't do anything to these men because they're guests of mine."

But mob rule prevailed and they all shouted, "Get out of the way. Who do you think you are? You're an outsider who's come here to live and now you want to stand in judgment of us. We'll treat you worse than we treat them."

And they rushed him and tried to break the door down. The two men inside opened the door just enough to reach out and pull Lot in to safety and then slammed it in the faces of the irate, sex-hungry men. The two men, or obvious angels as we're about to see, then struck the men closest to the entrance blind so they couldn't find the door. The angels turned to Lot and asked, "Do you have anyone here who belongs to you? Any family you want saved? Like maybe sons or daughters or sons-in-law? If you do, go get them and get them out of here because we're about to flatten this place like unleavened bread. Because of the rampant sin in this town, God has sent us to destroy it."

So, Lot found his chance and sneaked out and found his sons-in-law-to-be and told them, "You got to get out of here. God is about to destroy the place." But the sons-in-law-to-be just smiled and sneered at him because they thought he was joking.

Then dawn came and it was soon evident that there was no joke left in Sodom. The angels yelled to Lot, "Hurry up! Take your wife and two daughters and get out of here and be quick about it."

For a second, Lot hesitated. Evil as it was, it was still home and had been for many years and he had become somewhat of a local celebrity being on the city council and all and he just couldn't make himself go without a little twinge of regret. The two angels grabbed him by the hand and took his wife's hand and his daughters and led them to the outskirts of town. Then they commanded them, "Run! Run for your lives! And don't stop! And don't look back! Keep running till you get to the mountains or you, too, will be destroyed."

But Lot said, "Wait a minute, please. You've shown great kindness to me and I'm thankful that you have had mercy on me, but I can't run to those mountains. This whole thing, however you're going to destroy the city, will overcome me before I get there and I'll be dead long before I'm in the mountains. There's a little town just down the road. Let us run down there. We'll be safe down there."

Being a good host is not the only thing Lot inherited from old Abraham. Standing toe to toe and arguing with heavenly bodies must have been in the gene pool, also. He just could not do what he was told to do. He had to bargain and argue and do it his way.

And sure enough, the angel of God finally said, "Okay, okay. I won't touch that little town down the road, but get there fast because I can't do anything here till you do."

By the time the sun had come up that morning, Lot and his family had run safely to the small town of Zoar. And when they reached it, God, always as good as His word, rained down searing brimstone and hot fire from heaven. The entire plain and everything that grew there was a roaring blaze and it lit up the sky for miles and miles. And the sight was too great to ignore. Or maybe there was a little touch of longing to go back and maybe even a little pang of sorrow in leaving. But whatever the reason, Lot's wife looked back. The angels had warned her not to do this. One should never look back on an old sin. Leave it. Turn your face from it and never revisit it. But Lot's wife looked back, and she was turned into a pillar of salt.

It was early the next morning when Abraham got up and walked down the road to the spot where he had last talked to God. He looked way off across the plains toward Sodom and Gomorrah and he could see smoke rising up in the horizon like smoke from a chimney. But this smoke was from sin burning, not kindling wood.

God had destroyed both cities just as He told Abraham He would. And He had saved his blood-nephew. He destroyed the cities because He couldn't find ten good people. He did find four, so he led them to safety — three to safety anyway — and did what he had to do.

This, unfortunately, was not the end of Lot's story. There was a little more to come and a more appalling story you'll not find in all the pages of Scriptures.

In time, Lot and his two daughters left Zoar and headed up into the mountains to live. They settled in a cave and made it their home. One day the older daughter said to the younger daughter, "There is not a man anywhere close around here. Everybody else in the world has a man except us. If we're ever going to have children and families of our own, there is only one way. We have to get the old man drunk and sleep with him or we'll never have any kids."

So that night they hauled out the wine and got Lot out-of-his-mind drunk and the older girl went in the cave and lay down beside him and poor ole Lot never knew what happened.

The next night they did the same thing. They got their father sloppy drunk and this time the younger girl went in and lay down with him and again he never knew what he had done.

Both daughters conceived and gave birth. One son was named Moab and he was the father of all the Moabites. The other was named Ben-Ammi and he was the father of the Ammonites. And Lot, the father and grandfather of both of these boys, was never heard from again. We don't know how or where he died. Abraham never mentions him again. What his story means is up to the reader. He was a man caught up in circumstances of his own choosing. A man of some standing in his community. A man willing to sell his daughters in place of his guests. A man unable to convince his sons-in-law-to-be he was serious in a time of great danger. A man who argued with God in the face of disaster and changed His mind. And a man who got drunk and slept with his daughters. And that is about all there is to say about Lot, but there is still plenty more to come about Uncle Abraham and Aunt Sarah.

ABRAHAM IV

Abraham was on the move again. This time he wound up in Gerar, a town southwest of Mamre. And he pulled almost the same stunt he pulled in Egypt years before in telling everyone that Sarah was his sister and not his wife.

We have discussed the apparent striking beauty of Sarah but if we are to believe the Scriptures are true chronologically, then we're talking about a 90-year-old pregnant woman here. He was still afraid that she would be so irresistible to the powers-that-be that he should disguise their relationship for his own safety. And you know what? He was right.

Abimelech, king of Gerar, sent for her and took her into his household. And it wasn't long before Abimelech got a visit from God in a dream.

"Abimelech, you're a dead man. This woman you've taken is a married woman."

"Lord, I didn't touch her. I promise you I didn't. That man told me she was his sister. What I did I did with a clear conscience. My hands are clean."

"I know that," the Lord said. "I didn't let you touch her. Now send her back to this man, Abraham, because he's a prophet and he'll pray for you and you'll live. But if you don't send her back, you and all your family will die."

Abimelech wasted no time. Early the next morning he called all his people together and told them what had happened and they were scared to death. Next he called Abraham in and said, "What have you done to me? What would make you do such a thing to put my very life in danger like this?"

"Well," said Abraham, scrambling around for words, "you know, I figured this wasn't a very godly town and I was afraid you might kill me if you wanted her and thought she was my wife, so I just, you know . . . hey, but I didn't really lie. She is my half-sister. So it wasn't a total lie. So whenever we travel, I just tell everybody she's my sister."

And then the same thing happened again that happened

in Egypt. Abimelech gave Abraham sheep and cattle and men and women servants and told him he could live anywhere he wanted. And he went to Sarah and said, "I'm giving your brother a thousand pieces of silver." And Abimelech, the king, who was wronged, paid for Abraham's lie just as the pharaoh had.

Then Abraham prayed for Abimelech, that he and his wife and his maids would all be healed because when this whole episode started, God had closed the wombs of every woman in Abimelech's house, so that no children could be conceived. And all of this was done because of the Sarah incident.

Abraham lies, Abimelech pays. Sarah lies, Abimelech's wife suffers. When God is on your side, it doesn't matter who else is against you.

The Lord came to visit Sarah just as he said he would and she gave birth to a son and after eight days he was circumcised. And Sarah, in her happiness said, "God has made me laugh and everyone who hears about this will laugh with me. Who would have thought that I would give 100-year-old Abraham a son?"

And they named him, according to God's command, Isaac, which means "he laughs."

Isaac grew and was weaned and his father threw a big feast in celebration. But Sarah, still sensitive to an old hurt, noticed that Ishmael, Hagar the maid's son, was mocking and making fun of young Isaac. Sarah went to Abraham and said, "Get rid of that woman and her son and I mean it. He is not going to share in any inheritance with our son Isaac."

This was not easy on old Abraham. Both boys were his sons and he fretted over it and lost sleep over it. But God stepped in and took the matter in hand. "Abraham," said

God, "don't worry about all this. Do what Sarah tells you. I'll make Ishmael into a great nation, but Isaac is the one your lineage will pass through."

So the next morning, Abraham gathered food and water and sent Hagar and Ishmael, who was about 15 years old by now, on their way into the desert. When the water was gone, she put her son under a bush and went off by herself and sat down and cried because she couldn't bear to watch him die.

But God heard the boy crying and He spoke to Hagar. "What's wrong with you, Hagar? Don't be afraid. I heard the boy crying. Get up and take him by the hand. I'm going to make him into a great nation."

And at that moment, God opened Hagar's eyes and she saw a well and she ran and filled up her bottle and gave Ishmael a drink. And God remained with the boy through the years as he grew. He became an archer and in time his mother went down to Egypt and found him a wife.

Abraham lived in sometimes-unfriendly lands and with sometimes-unfriendly and ungodly people. But he "bargained and bartered" and "wheeled and dealed" and survived by the grace of God. It was God who protected him and God who tested him. Not unlike our own relationship with God today, only we have probably not been tested as Abraham was tested.

"Abraham," God called.

"Here I am, Lord."

"Take your only son, Isaac, whom I know you really love, and go to Moriah and offer him up as a burnt sacrifice on one of the mountains I'll point out later."

Now Abraham had argued with God on how many good people it would take to save an evil city, but here he never said a word. The old fire was either gone or his faith was tenfold stronger. He got up early the next morning, saddled up his donkey, called two of his servants along with Isaac, went out and cut wood for the offering and then set out on the journey.

They had been traveling for three days when Abraham looked up and saw the mountain off in the distance. He stopped and told the two servants, "Stay here with the donkey. The boy and I will be back in a minute."

Abraham gathered up the wood and put it in Isaac's arms. He carried the fire and the knife himself. As they walked up the mountainside, Isaac was the first to speak. "Father, we have the wood and the knife and the fire, but where's the lamb?"

Without looking at his son, Abraham trudged on, simply and profoundly saying, "God will provide the lamb."

When they reached the top, Abraham built an altar and arranged the wood on it. Then he took his son and tied him up and laid him on top of the wood. And then, as a final sign to his faith in God, he raised the knife.

"Abraham! Abraham!"

"Here I am."

"Don't lay a hand on that boy." It was the voice of an angel of God. "You have passed the test and now I know you do truly fear the Lord. You were about to kill your one and only son in the name of God."

A rustling sound from behind him made Abraham turn around quickly. And there he saw a ram with his horns caught in the brush. He walked over to him, with knife in hand, and offered a burnt sacrifice to the Lord. And he named the mountain on which he was standing Jehovah-jireh, "the Lord will provide."

Then the angel called from heaven one more time and assured Abraham he had passed the test and assured him again that his descendants would be as numerous as the stars and that all nations on earth would be blessed because of what he had been willing to do there that day.

Isaac was alive. Abraham was assured his place in history and in heaven. Life was good. God is good.

Sarah, beautiful and lovely Sarah, the love of Abraham's life, died at the age of 127 years. Abraham mourned her. He wept over her. They had made many memories together and had seen many wonderful and miraculous things together. They'd been in trouble together and in danger together and most of all in love together. But the time had come to bury the woman and the memories. She had died in Hebron, so Abraham went to the Hittites and said, "I'm a stranger in your land. My wife has died. Sell me some land so that I can bury my dead."

"No sir, Abraham. You're a prince to us. You just pick any tomb you want and it's yours. No charge at all."

"Well, I appreciate that," said Abraham, "but if you're willing to give me a tomb then maybe you're willing to speak on my behalf to Ephron who owns the cave of Machpelah at the end of his field. That is really the burial place I want and tell him I'll pay full price for it."

Ephron was in earshot of Abraham's offer and he jumped up immediately and spoke so that everyone could hear. "Listen to me. I give you the field. I give you the cave. Take it. It's yours. Get outta here."

"No," insisted Abraham, "I'll pay you full price."

"Listen to me," Ephron said waving his hand in the air. "The land is worth 400 shekels. What's 400 shekels among friends? Take it. Go on. Bury your dead."

ABRAHAM • 35

So Abraham paid him the suggested 400 shekels, about 20 of our dollars, and we have just witnessed maybe the earliest "art of the deal" in history. The exchange was pure deal making. All business. And Ephron was a slick one.

Abraham now owned both the field and the cave of Machpelah and this is where he laid his beloved Sarah to rest.

Abraham was old and tired. If Sarah died at 127, that made him 137 and it was time to be tired and to wind down. But he had one more thing he wanted to do. He wanted to find the proper wife for his son Isaac. As was the custom, this was his duty and he had definite ideas about how he should go about it.

He called his oldest and most loyal servant in and said to him, "Place your hand under my thigh. Now I want you to swear by God in heaven that you will get a wife for my son but that you will not get one from here in Canaan. I want you to swear that you will go back to my home country, among my relatives, and find a wife for Isaac."

Marrying foreigners was not an acceptable thing to do. Many foreigners did not worship God and to marry a heathen woman was more than just frowned upon. They would rather marry family than foreigners.

The servant, serious about his charge, asked, "What if the woman won't come back here. Do I take Isaac back to your country to live there?"

"No, no. Absolutely not," Abraham said adamantly. "Make sure you never take my son back there. The Lord gave us this land and He gave it to Isaac as my only son. If the woman is not willing to come here, then you're out from under the oath. But whatever you do, don't take Isaac back there."

And just before the old and faithful servant put his hand

under Abraham's thigh and swore the oath, Abraham assured him, "The Lord will send an angel before you to show you who the right woman is." And the servant took the oath and then packed ten camels and set out to do what his master had commanded.

His commission was successful and he brought home Isaac's first cousin once-removed to be his wife. How it all happened was a fantastic story, but it's Isaac's story and one we'll leave to be told under his banner.

But Abraham's tale was not completely told and his life was not nearly over. He remarried. He took a wife named Keturah and she bore him six, (count 'em, six) more sons. Zimran, Jokshan, Medan, Midian, Ishbak, and Shuah.

And while he was still alive, he gave them their inheritance and sent them away to make lives for themselves in other lands. God only recognized one son, and in the end so did Abraham, because when he died he left everything he owned to Isaac.

Abraham gave up the ghost and died at a good old age of 175 years. And at the end, something happened that might have surprised even the old patriarch himself. Of all his sons, only two came to bury him. Isaac and Ishmael. They took him to the cave of Machpelah and buried him beside his Sarah. And they were finally at peace together.

So on which side of the fence does this good man of God fall? He had faith but he had doubts. He was honest yet deceitful. He stumbled but God caught him.

Hero or outlaw, where does he fall?
Right on the fence with the rest of us all.

 # JOSEPH

Genesis 37–50

There are ten men named Joseph in the Bible, five in the Old Testament and five in the New. The most famous in the New is, of course, Joseph, the earthly father of Jesus and the most famous in the Old is Joseph, son of Jacob, grandson of Isaac, great-grandson of Abraham. How's that for a lineage?

Rather impressive, I think, and this particular Joseph is our man of the moment.

Joseph's story starts when he was 17 years old, but to really understand him and who he was, let's look a little bit at his family. You hear about your dysfunctional families of the 21st century, but few compare to this clan of the 16th century B.C. Joseph had ten half-brothers, one half-sister, and one full brother. Six of his half-brothers and his half sister belonged to his father's *other* wife, two half-brothers belonged to one of the maids and two belonged to another of the maids. Joseph was next to the youngest and his only full brother, Benjamin, *was* the youngest. Now there is a family to sit down to supper with.

Joseph's mother was named Rachel and in all honesty was the only woman his father, Jacob, really loved. Rachel was his favorite wife and thus Joseph and Benjamin were his favorite sons. So with all of this in mind, it will make the rest of the story easier to understand because father Jacob was not above showing favoritism among his boys.

Seventeen years old and out in the fields with his ten older brothers, Joseph had a tendency to be a little tattle-tale. He would tell his father everything in the evening that happened that day and every little thing the older brothers did and said, and it got to be a pretty bad rub between the boys and the kid. And to top it all off, father Jacob made young Joseph a beautiful, rich-looking coat that the Scriptures call "a coat of many colors," and he strutted around in it until his half-brothers hated him and couldn't find it in themselves to even speak a kind word to him.

Joseph was a dreamer and working in the fields one day he told his brothers about a dream he had had the night before. He said, "We were all working out here in the field, tying up sheaves of grain when all of a sudden my sheaf rose up and stood upright and all of your sheaves gathered around and bowed down to mine."

Now this is not the type of thing you share with people who already hate you, but Joseph was either oblivious to their feelings or didn't care about them at all. Or maybe he was just being honest. Or maybe he was rubbing some salt in where it hurt the most. Whatever the case, the brothers didn't find the dream very funny or very endearing. It just caused them to hate him all the more.

And wouldn't you know, here came Joseph in a few days with the story of another dream. He told his brothers, "I dreamed this time that the sun and the moon and 11 stars were bowing down to me." Boy, ole Joseph, 1 of 12 brothers, sure knew how to keep the family fires stirred up.

The older 10 brothers (young Benjamin was usually back at the house) were sent off by their father to tend flocks of sheep near a neighboring town. After a while, we don't know how long, Jacob sent Joseph out to check on his siblings and told him to report back as to how they were doing. So off he went, with his pretty coat, on a mission for his father. He searched for a while, asked directions, and finally could see them way off in the distance. And just as he could see them sitting there in the pasture, they could see him, far off, walking slowly toward them. And they looked at one another and said, "Here comes that dreamer. When he gets here, let's kill him!"

"Yeah," another one said. "Let's throw him down in one of those cisterns and we'll tell daddy that a wild animal attacked him. Then we won't hear about any more dreams of his."

Reuben, the oldest brother, said, "Hold up guys. Grab him and throw him in the cistern if you want to, but don't kill him. We don't want the blood of our brother on our hands."

So they sat and watched him get closer and closer and as he got right on them and was about to speak to them, they grabbed him and stripped his coat of many colors off his back and threw him in a cistern. There was no water in this particular cistern, so what it amounted to was a big hole in the ground.

Reuben, who either had no stomach for practical jokes or who really was busy with his work, was off somewhere with his duties that evening when the others sat down in the grass to eat supper. They heard a rumbling noise and looked up to see a caravan of merchants rounding the bend with a line of camels loaded down with spices and balm and myrrh and heading for the market down in Egypt.

A smile came over brother Judah's face. He had an idea. He said in a low voice to his other brothers, "Reuben doesn't want us to kill him, so how about this? We stop the caravan and sell him to them and they can take him into Egypt and sell him on the slave market and that way his blood is not on our hands and everybody's happy."

Sounded like a good idea to the rest of the family, so they pulled Joseph out of his hole and for one fleeting moment must have given him hope that his nightmare was about to end. But he was helpless as he watched them sell him for 20 pieces of silver to the caravan of merchants. (Roughly, the 20 pieces of silver amounted to $12.80, so there was more revenge than profit in the whole ordeal.)

The real scene came when Reuben showed up back in camp that evening and went over to the cistern, looked down in it, and failed to see his little brother. He challenged the other nine with, "What do we do now?" And after a little thought and plotting, they came up with the perfect scheme. They had kept Joseph's coat, so they simply killed a goat and smeared blood all over the jacket and made the journey back to their father's house with a pat story he could never doubt.

Handing it to him with bowed heads, they said, "We found this along the road. Is this the coat of your son?"

The old man held the beautiful, bloodied robe in his hands and shook his head. "Yes. Apparently some wild animal tore young Joseph to pieces and devoured him." And Jacob wept and went into such a deep mourning that he refused to be comforted. "I will go to my grave mourning my son," he said, and he wept some more.

JOSEPH II

A Jew in Egypt did not hold much social status, especially one who probably arrived in chains and was offered for sale to the highest bidder. But as *luck* would have it, the highest bidder turned out to be a man named Potiphar who was at least a respecter of God, if not totally God-fearing. He was also captain of the guard, one of Pharaoh's right-hand men. He took Joseph home with him to live in his house with his family and in time, seeing that Joseph was a good and trustworthy man, put him in charge of everything he owned. So you see "luck" had nothing to do with it. The Lord was looking after Joseph after all.

Potiphar profited and succeeded in everything he did under the management of Joseph and their relationship was solid and reliable. But one part of Potiphar's life was not under Joseph's watchful eye; and that was his marriage.

His wife had a roving and wandering eye and the Scriptures tell us in no unclear terms that Joseph was a handsome and well-built man. This fact did not go unnoticed by Potiphar's wife and one day she came on to him in no unclear way. She said, "Come and go to bed with me."

Joseph turned her down. He said, "How could I do something like that to Potiphar when he has put all his trust in me. It would be a sin against Potiphar and against God."

This rejection had little effect on her. She continued her pursuit by hounding him constantly. And just as constantly, he turned her down.

But you know what they say about a woman scorned. And she waited her time. She waited for a day when all the other servants were out of the house and she grabbed Joseph by his coat sleeve and begged him one last time, "Come to bed with me now."

Joseph pulled away from her and, doing so, slid right out of his coat and left her holding it as he ran out of the house. It seems Joseph's coats were always getting him in trouble, and this time again the evidence was in the wrong hands because Potiphar's wife yelled rape. Literally, yelled rape. She screamed for the servants to come running and told them how "that little Hebrew" had come into her bedroom and "look, I still have his coat" and how she had screamed and had run him out of the house.

She was still holding the coat when Potiphar came in that evening and she relished in relating the same tale to him. Potiphar's anger was understandable and he did what any good husband with his power would do; he had Joseph put in prison.

So Joseph, the Jewish slave in Egypt, the one over whom God was watching, was in a bind again. But even in prison we see God really was watching because the warden took a liking to young Joseph and made him a trustee and put him in charge of all the other prisoners. And this was the break that Joseph needed.

Now it seems the king's butler and baker had been thrown in prison for offenses to the crown of some sort or another and the inside network drew them in close contact to Joseph. He noticed one day that they were both wearing long faces and asked them what was wrong.

"We both had dreams last night," they said, "and we don't have anyone who can interpret them for us."

With a confidence that only comes from God, Joseph said, "Tell me your dreams. God can interpret them for you through me."

So the butler began, "I dreamed there was a vine with three branches and grapes bloomed on the branches and I squeezed the juice from the grapes and put it in Pharaoh's cup and put the cup in Pharaoh's hand."

"This is what it means," Joseph said. "The three branches represent three days. And in three days Pharaoh will restore you to your old position and you will be putting cups in his hand as his butler, just like you did in the old days."

The butler was elated and while Joseph still had him happy, he said, "And when you're out of here and back in the king's good graces, don't forget me. Mention my name to Pharaoh and get me out of this prison."

The baker, having watched all this from a distance, said, "Hey, I had a dream, too, remember. In my dream I had three baskets of bread on my head. It was the king's bread and the birds kept flying down and picking at it and eating the bread."

"Okay, this is what that means," Joseph said. "The three baskets represent three days, and in three days Pharaoh will cut off your head and hang your carcass on a tree and the birds will eat your flesh to the bone." Not the news the baker was looking for.

In three days it was Pharaoh's birthday and he held a feast for all his officials.

On that day at the celebration he restored the butler to his old position and hanged the baker just as Joseph had predicted. The baker was dead and the butler, back home and in the comfort and security of his old surroundings, forgot all about the Jewish boy in prison and the promise he had made him.

It seemed to Joseph that not only the butler but also God had forgotten him.

Two years passed and this time the dreamer was Pharaoh

himself. He dreamed he was standing by the Nile when seven fat cows came out of the water and grazed on the banks. Then seven ugly, gaunt cows came out and stood beside them and ate the seven fat cows. Then Pharaoh woke up.

He fell asleep again and had another dream immediately. Seven big ears of corn grew on one stalk. Then seven thin ears grew on it and devoured the seven good ones. Then he awoke again.

He felt these dreams meant something important, but for the life of him he couldn't figure it out on his own. He sent for magicians and wise men but none of them could help solve the mystery of the dreams. Pharaoh was troubled and bothered. The butler, who had been privy to all of this, finally came to the king and said, "I've just remembered something. Back when you put the baker and me in prison a couple of years ago, we had dreams we couldn't figure out. There was a young Hebrew in there with us who interpreted them for us and he was right on the money. I think he's still there in the prison. Shall I get him?"

This was an answer to both Pharaoh's and Joseph's prayers. He was sent for and after he cleaned up, shaved, and changed clothes he was led into the royal chambers of the king.

Pharaoh looked down at him and said, "I had a dream. Two actually. And I hear you can tell me what they mean."

"I can't," Joseph said, "but God can. Tell me your dreams."

So Pharaoh told him about the seven thin cows eating the seven fat ones and about the seven thin ears of corn eating the seven good ones, and then he waited for the Jewish convict to give him answers that would salve his soul.

Joseph looked him in the eye. "Your dreams are one

and the same. God has warned you of what he is about to do. There will be seven years of plenty throughout Egypt followed by seven years of famine. The reason he gave you two dreams meaning the same thing is to show you that he has already made up his mind on the matter and it will happen soon. I suggest you find a wise man and put him in charge of all of Egypt. Appoint commissioners under him all over the land and see that a fifth of all of the harvests during the seven good years is stored and saved in reserve for the coming seven lean years. If you don't, the famine will destroy the entire country."

This seemed like a good plan to Pharaoh and he went to his council with it. He asked them whom they should select as an overseer and prompted them that it should be a man of God. Then, as if listening to his own heart, he said, "How about you, Joseph? You already have this special relationship with God. I'll make you the head man in my palace and over all of Egypt. Only one man will be greater than you and that will be me."

And he took his signet ring and put it on Joseph's finger. He dressed him in linen robes and put a gold chain around his neck. He gave him his own private chariot and wherever he went, men shouted, "Make way." And he even gave him an Egyptian name and an Egyptian wife. Joseph was a big man in Egypt. Second only to the king. And he was only 30 years old.

Joseph took his work very seriously. In the next seven years he traveled the country extensively and saw that so much food and grain was stored in each city that they finally just quit keeping records. What was stored was beyond measure. In his personal life, he also flourished. Two sons were born to him and life was good.

Then came the seven years of famine. The people were desperate just as Joseph had predicted they would be and they came to Pharaoh, hungry, just as he predicted. But he had storehouses full of food to sell them and see them through the bad years. And not just Egypt. All the surrounding countries were crushed by the same famine. And they all came and Joseph, because of the dream that God had sent Pharaoh, was prepared to help them.

JOSEPH III

Joseph's father and brothers were still living back in Canaan, which had been hit pretty hard by the famine, also. Jacob heard there was plenty of grain and food for sale in Egypt and decided to send some of his sons to check it out.

"What are you sitting around here looking at each other for? Get up and head down to Egypt and get us something to eat or we're all going to just sit here and die."

So ten of Joseph's brothers, Reuben, Simeon, Levi, Judah, Dan, Naphtali, Gad, Asher, Issachar, and Zebulun went on a food-buying journey into Egypt. Their father, Jacob, wouldn't let his youngest son, Benjamin, go for fear that something would happen to him.

When the brothers ten arrived, they were instructed to go to the governor of the land who would take care of selling them everything they needed. This governor was, of course, brother Joseph but they didn't recognize him. He was at least 40 years old now and they hadn't seen him since he was 17. But he knew them. And when they bowed down before him and stated their needs, he decided not to give his hand away at the present. Flashes from nearly a quarter of a century ago of that hole in the ground and that caravan and the coat of many colors must have gone through his mind and he pretended to be the stranger they thought he was.

"Where are you men from?" Joseph asked.

"We're from Canaan. We came down to buy food."

"I don't believe you. I think you're spies and you've come to case our nation and our border security." Joseph was having fun now and he was remembering the dreams he had had years ago and shared with his brothers. The one about the 12 sheaves and how his had risen up and all the others gathered round and bowed down to his; and the one about the sun and the moon and the 11 stars and how they had all bowed down in front of him. His dreams were coming true right before his eyes and he was going to enjoy every minute of it.

"No, no, my lord," they all cried. "We are your humble servants. We've only come to buy food. We're honest men. We're not spies. As a matter of fact, we're all the sons of one man; a family."

"No, I don't believe you." Joseph wasn't giving an inch.

"We promise you what we say is true. We are a family of 12 brothers. The youngest brother is back in Canaan with our father and we have one brother who is dead." They were scared.

"No, I think you're all spies. And as a test, you will not leave here until your youngest brother comes here in person. I think I might send one of you back to Canaan to get him and hold the rest of you here. And if he never comes, then I'll know for sure you're spies. Yes, that's what I'll do. But in the meantime, I'm going to throw all ten of you in jail." And he did.

For three days he kept them in jail and then went to them and said, "I'm a God-fearing man. I want to do what's fair. Instead of keeping nine of you in prison and sending one back for your brother, I'll keep one of you and send the nine back. That way the nine can take grain back to your starving families and if you're honest people, you'll come back for your brother and bring your youngest one with you."

Much of this change of heart had to be for his father, Jacob, and for the long desire to see his only full brother, Benjamin, again.

The ten brothers looked at one another ashamedly and talked among themselves, "We're being punished by God for what we did to our brother years ago. Remember how he begged and pleaded with us for his life before we sold him to that caravan? But we ignored his crying and now all of this trouble is coming down on us because of what we did."

They spoke freely among themselves in their own language not knowing there was anyone about who could understand them. Not knowing that the brother they were speaking of was standing among them as an Egyptian and hearing and comprehending every word they said. And as that brother listened, he turned away from them and cried. Joseph, the second-man-in-charge in all of Egypt, cried as his brothers talked, but they didn't see him.

He turned back around and gave orders for Simeon to be tied and bound and put back in prison as the hostage brother to guarantee their return. And then he gave orders to have nine sacks filled with grain and packed for the journey and, unbeknownst to the brothers, he had their money packed in with the grain – money they had brought to buy food, money that had been taken from them when they were imprisoned.

That night they stopped at an inn and when one of the brothers dug down in his sack for grain to feed the donkeys, he found his money. And all the brothers were confused and scared. They said to each other, "What has God done to us? What is happening?"

They arrived in Canaan at the home of their father and they told him everything that had happened to them since they left home. How they had been accused of being spies; how they had been in prison, how Simeon was being held hostage; and how they had to take Benjamin back with them to prove they weren't spies. They unpacked as they told their story and there in each pack of grain was each brother's money just as the one brother had found his at the inn.

They were scared all over again and so was the old man.

Jacob said, "My sons keep losing my sons. Joseph is no more. Simeon is no more and now you want to take Benjamin. No, absolutely not. It would kill me if something happened to my baby son Benjamin."

Reuben, the oldest, said, "Father, if we don't bring him back to you safely, you can kill *my* two sons. Trust me and I promise we'll bring him back."

The old man, Jacob, now called Israel, looked at his sons with sad and aging eyes and said, "No."

The famine continued and became more severe with each passing day. When the grain they had brought up from Egypt was gone, Jacob told them to go back down there and buy some more food.

Judah, his number four son, said, "Dad, we told you we can't do that. If we go back down there without Benjamin, we're all dead meat. This governor means business."

Jacob said, "Why did you even tell him you had a younger brother at home?"

"He grilled us," they all replied. "He just kept on asking us questions. He asked if our father was living and if we

had another brother. We simply answered his questions."
(The only question Joseph asked them was, "Where are
you men from?" Everything they told him, they told out
of fear.)

Judah finally said to his father, "Let me take the boy
with me as my personal responsibility. If I don't bring him
back and stand him here in front of you, I'll bear the blame
for it for the rest of my life. We have to do this or we're all
going to starve. And we have to do it now. We could have
been down there and back twice in this time."

So again, Jacob looked at his sons with sad and aging
eyes and said, "Okay, but take some gifts. Fill your bags
with ointments and honey and spices and myrrh. Take him
some pistachio nuts and some almonds. And take double
the money back with you. Give him back what you found in
your grain sacks in case it was a mistake and then you'll still
have money to buy food. And take care of your little brother
and bring him and Simeon home with you."

So the ten brothers left a sad old father on the doorstep
and hurried down to the land of Egypt on the adventure of
their lives.

They arrived and found Joseph and presented themselves to him but he didn't speak a word to them. He turned
to his butler and said, "Take these men to my house and
kill a calf and prepare a feast. They're going to have lunch
with me at noon." Then he left and waited for all this to
happen.

When the brothers realized they were being taken to
the governor's house, they got scared again. They were afraid
they were going to be accused of stealing the money they
had found in their packs, so they pulled the butler aside and
pleaded their case to him. The butler was reassuring as he

told them, "Don't be afraid. God put that money in your sacks." And then he went and got their brother Simeon and brought him out to them.

The butler took them into Joseph's house and gave them water to wash with and saw that their animals were fed and bedded. The 11 brothers laid out the gifts they had brought Joseph and awaited his arrival at noon.

Joseph walked in and they all bowed down before him and presented him the gifts. Without acknowledging them, he asked, "How is your father? Is he still living?"

"Yes. He's alive and well."

Then he looked down at Benjamin, his only full brother. His mother's only other son. "Is this your youngest brother? The one you told me about?"

But before they could even answer him, he turned and rushed out of the room. He went into his private quarters and sobbed. The years and the memories and the moment at hand were too much for the man all of Egypt looked up to. He cried and dried his tears and washed his face and came out in full control of himself and gave the command to his staff to serve the food.

Joseph was served alone. His brothers were served separately. And the Egyptians, who were dining with them, were served separately. All of this because an Egyptian would not eat with a Hebrew even if they were a guest or even if they were second-in-charge in all the land.

Joseph's brothers were seated in order of their ages and when they realized this, they were amazed by it and certainly thought it was a coincidence. But what amazed them more was that when they were served, Benjamin's portions were five times as much as anyone else's.

They feasted and drank freely and had a great time and

the 12 brothers were finally under the same roof again, but only Joseph knew it.

But all of this is not to be misunderstood. Joseph was not through toying with his brothers. They had harmed and scarred him years ago and his revenge was not yet fulfilled. After the meal he instructed his trusty butler to fill their individual sacks again with all the food they would hold and stuff their money back in there again and then he added a new touch to the proceedings. He told his servant to place his own (Joseph's) valued silver cup in Benjamin's sack. This was done without any of them knowing of it and at first light the next day, the 11 took off for home.

Joseph gave them a small head start and then called for his butler. "Go after them and search their packs and see which one stole my prized silver cup. I can't believe they would trade evil for the kindness I have shown them."

The servant took off after them and Joseph stood and watched with a sly smile on his face.

The brothers were stopped and asked and accused and registered shock that anyone would think they would do such a thing. They said, "We even brought money back we found in our sacks by mistake. Why would we steal from your master's house? Search us and if you find it, the one who has it will die and the rest of us will become your slaves."

The butler said, "Whoever has it will become my slave. The rest of you will be free to go." And he searched their sacks, starting with Reuben the oldest and going down the line until he got to Benjamin, the youngest. And there in his sack was the cup of Joseph.

The brothers tore at their clothes in disbelief and agony. But they didn't leave without their youngest brother. They loaded up their donkeys and returned to the city with him.

They went to Joseph's house and threw themselves on the ground in front of him and Joseph shamed them. "What have you done? Don't you know that a man like me can find out things by divination?"

The brothers said, "What can we do? How can we prove our innocence? If we can't we will all stay and be your slaves."

"Far be it from me to do such a thing to all of you. I will only make the guilty one my slave. The rest of you can go back to your father." Joseph played a hard game.

Then Judah, the fourth oldest, stepped forward and gave the speech of his life. He laid his heart out at the feet of Joseph and invited him to stomp it in the ground. He spoke sincerely, not knowing he was speaking to his own blood. "My lord, please don't be angry with us. When we first came to you, you asked if we had a father. You asked if we had a brother. We told you we had an aged father and a young brother and a brother who is dead. You demanded we bring the young brother so you could see him even though we told you it would kill our father to be separated from him. We left and you held a brother hostage.

"When we left home to return here this time, our father resisted us bringing young Benjamin. He said to us, 'One son, of the wife whom I love dearly, has already gone from me and been torn to bits and if you take this boy and harm comes to him, my old gray head will go down to the grave in misery.'

"So you see, my lord, if we go home without this boy, our father will surely die. So, I beg you, please, let me remain here in place of the boy and let him go home with his brothers to see his father."

Was it the words of Judah that touched Joseph? Was it the weight of the guilt of revenge? Was it seeing a brother grovel at his feet? Or was it purely and gloriously the hand of God reaching in and saying, "Enough"?

Joseph, the Hebrew Egyptian, was moved. When Judah was through, he could no longer control himself. He cried out, "Clear the room. Everybody out of here except these men from Canaan!"

And when the room was cleared and there was no one but the brothers, Joseph wept. He wept so loudly he could be heard throughout Pharaoh's palace.

Through his tears he faced his brothers and said, "I am Joseph. Is my father alive?"

The brothers were dumbstruck and terrified. "Come closer to me," Joseph said. "I'm your brother. The one you sold to Egypt. But don't worry. Don't be scared. And don't be angry at yourselves because it wasn't you who did it, it was God. God sent me ahead to Egypt to prepare for this famine and to save your lives and the lives of your families. God made me lord of Pharaoh's house. All of this was God's plan and for the good of God.

"Now go back home and tell our father that God has made me lord over all of Egypt. And tell him to come down here to live. Bring the children and bring the grandchildren and all the flocks and herds and be close to me for there are still five more years of famine.

"Now go quickly and tell Father what you have seen and what I have told you because I am your brother, Joseph."

And he grabbed Benjamin and hugged him and wept. Then he kissed each brother and wept with them. And they all talked together as brothers should.

When the news reached Pharaoh, he was elated. He gave the brothers pack animals to take back to Canaan and instructed them to bring their father and families back and promised to give them the best land Egypt had to offer. He gave them carts to haul their children and wives and told them to never mind about their belongings as he would give them all new things when they got back to Egypt.

Joseph, on the authority of the pharaoh, sent ten donkeys loaded with corn and grain and bread and ten donkeys loaded with fineries to his father. To each brother he gave a new set of clothing. But to Benjamin he gave three hundred shekels of silver and *five* new sets of clothing. As they left, he waved them goodbye and admonished them in a brotherly way, "Don't fight among yourselves before you get home."

And when they arrived home and told Jacob about all that had happened, he was stunned and didn't believe them. But their repeated, "Joseph is alive!" finally sank in when he saw all the gifts and the carts Joseph had sent to carry him back to Egypt. The old man's spirit was revived. All he could say was, "My son Joseph is alive and I'm going to see him before I die."

JOSEPH IV

Jacob set out for Egypt. On the way, he stopped to offer sacrifices to God. And on one of these stops, God appeared to him in a night vision and spoke to him and called him Jacob. This was rather odd being as how God had changed his name to Israel years before and even told him that he would never be called Jacob again. That from that day forward he would always be known as Israel, which means "to struggle with God." But for some reason God wanted to call him Jacob on this particular night and if God wants to change His mind, who are we to question Him?

God said, "Jacob, I am God. The God of your father, Isaac. Don't be afraid to go down to Egypt. I know it has not always been the friendliest country to your people, but go and I will make you a great nation down there. Be assured that I will go to Egypt with you and I'll bring you back home again. And I promise you that Joseph's own hand will close your eyes when you lie down to die."

So old "Israel" headed for the land of Egypt with his entire clan — his sons and their sons and daughters and his daughters-in-law — and they numbered more than 70 in all. And they took their flocks of sheep and their herds of cattle and everything they owned on earth and traveled slowly down to a strange new home.

When they arrived, Israel sent his son Judah ahead to meet Joseph and to find out exactly where they were to settle. Joseph eagerly had his chariot readied and he and Judah rushed out to Goshen to meet the clan and to see his father whom he had not laid eyes on for over 20 years. And when they saw one another, they threw their arms around each other, father and son, and Joseph is said to have wept for a long, long time.

And seeing that his long-lost son was truly alive, Israel said, "Now I'm ready to die."

Joseph greeted all his brothers and their households and then gave them a few words of instructions before they went in to meet Pharaoh. "Now brothers, I'll go up and meet with Pharaoh and tell him my entire family has arrived from Canaan and has brought everything with them they own. I'll tell him you're here to stay and make this your new home. But there's one thing you must do when you're called in to meet him, and this is very important. When he asks you, 'What is your occupation?' say you tend cattle. Don't mention the sheep because Egyptians hate shepherds. And he'll never give you the prime fields to settle in if he thinks you're bringing sheep in. Shepherds around here are nomads who come and use the land and then go off somewhere else to do the same. So be sure now to say you're cattlemen."

When Joseph went off to meet with Pharaoh and to tell him the good news that his family had arrived safely, he took five of his brothers with him. He presented the five brothers to the court of Pharaoh and sure enough, the very first question Pharaoh asked them was, "What is your occupation?"

And in unison they answered, "We're shepherds."

They went on to say they had come to Egypt because their land was dried up and their grass was gone and they humbly begged to settle in Goshen, the richest and most desirable fields around. Joseph must have cringed and wondered why he was ever glad to see these bumbling, stupid brothers of his. He had instructed them in the ways of the world and they had proceeded to do exactly the opposite of what he had told them to do. Once a shepherd, always a shepherd.

But wait. Pharaoh turned out to be a better guy than Joseph had given him credit for being, because none of this fazed him at all. He welcomed them all with open arms — the whole family.

Then Joseph brought his father and presented him before Pharaoh. And Jacob, the lord of no land but ordained by God, blessed Pharaoh. Not the other way around. Not a king blessing a lowly shepherd, but the shepherd blessing the king. God's hand could plainly be seen in all this.

"How old are you?" Pharaoh asked.

"I'm 130 years old," Israel replied.

And then he went out to live with his family on the best

Egyptian land available. And his son Joseph, the second-in-charge, gave them all food and rations according to the number of their children.

The famine was even worse than expected. Joseph sold the people of Egypt grain until their money was all gone. Then they came to him and begged for his mercy. They admitted they were broke and asked for food. This was a hard thing to witness and hear, but Joseph kept a stone face and maybe a stone heart as he told them, "Go home and get your livestock if you have no money, and bring them here and I'll give you food in exchange."

So he gave them food in exchange for their cattle and their sheep and their goats and their donkeys. And he got them through the year without starving.

But when that year was over, they came back again and said, "We have nothing to sell or exchange except our bodies and our land. Give us food and we'll become servants and slaves to Pharaoh."

So Joseph bought up all the land in Egypt for the pharaoh. From one end of it to the other, he acquired their land and their bodies and lives. They were servants to the king. And even on this he put a stipulation. He told the people as he gave them seeds to plant, "When your crops come in, you owe one-fifth to Pharaoh." Taxes. One fifth goes to the government and that law still stands in Egypt today.

Joseph: a man of God, a hero to the people, and now an agent for the government. He wore many hats, some more respectable than others. Was he a hardened company man? Was he fearful of losing his position? Or was he, as some thought, just another arrogant ruler. To his mind he was just doing his job.

His father, Jacob, and his family were doing just fine.

They were out there in the land of Goshen where the grass was green and the water was blue and they were prospering and increasing greatly in number.

Jacob lived out there for 17 years, which made him 147 years old. He felt himself beginning to weaken and die, so he called for his son Joseph to come see him. He said, "Joseph, my boy, I have always found favor in your eyes. Put your hand under my thigh and make me a promise that you will take me home to bury me. Carry me out of Egypt and let me rest with my fathers where they're buried."

Joseph placed his hand under his father's thigh, a ritual Jacob's grandfather, Abraham, had originally requested, and promised his father that he would sleep with his fathers in his homeland.

"Swear to me, Joseph."

And Joseph swore.

The next time Joseph was called out to see his father, he was told that the old man was surely dying this time. So he took his two sons, Manasseh and Ephraim, along with him and the old man rallied and sat up in bed. Jacob said to Joseph, "I am going to adopt your two sons, my grandsons, as my own sons, thus leaving them full shares of my inheritance and legacy. They will be equal to Reuben and Simeon and Judah and all my other sons." (Instead of 12 tribes of Israel, now there would be 13 tribes, as Manasseh and Ephraim would share Joseph's portion.)

Jacob's eyes were failing him along with the rest of his body and as he looked at the three figures from the edge of his bed, he asked Joseph, "Who are these boys?"

"These are my sons, Father. Sons God has given me."

"Bring them closer so I can bless them," the old man said.

So Joseph brought the two boys closer so their grand-father could kiss them and hug them. Jacob, filled with emo-tion, said to his son, "I never expected to see your face again and now God has even allowed me to see the faces of your children." At this, Joseph bowed down in front of his father with his face to the ground.

Preparing for the blessing from Jacob and considering his father's aging eyes, Joseph, with his left hand, stood Manasseh in front of Jacob's right hand and with his right hand stood Ephraim in front of Jacob's left hand. This was according to tradition as the eldest was to be blessed with the right hand. But as Jacob reached out to bless them, he crossed his arms and put his right hand on Ephraim's head, which was the younger. He then put his left hand on Manasseh's head, the older.

When Joseph saw this happening, he was very upset. He reached out to change his father's hands and said, "No, Father. You have them mixed up. This is Manasseh, the first-born."

And Jacob, to his son's surprise, said, "I know, son. I know. He too will become great, but the younger boy will be greater. He will become the head of many nations."

And Israel blessed them that day, Ephraim ahead of Manasseh.

"Now Joseph I'm about to die. I want all my sons here."

And he called them all together and told them each what the future held in store for them. And he blessed them and gave them these instructions. "I am about to go and be with my fathers. Bury me with my family in the cave of Ephron the Hittite back in Canaan. In that cave is buried my grandparents Abraham and Sarah, my father and mother, Isaac and Rebekah, and my first wife, Leah."

And at this, the old patriarch drew his feet up in bed, breathed his last, and went to be with his fathers.

Joseph threw himself on his father and cried and kissed him for the last time. He ordered the physicians to embalm the body and to take the full 40 days that was required for a proper embalming. And then all of Egypt mourned him for 70 days.

After the mourning period, Joseph went to Pharaoh and told him about the promise he had made to his father and how he had assured him on his deathbed that he would personally take him home to Canaan to be buried. He, in turn, promised Pharaoh that he would return when the duty was done.

So Joseph, along with his brothers and dignitaries from Pharaoh's court, traveled to Canaan with chariots and horsemen. When they reached the Jordan, they stopped and mourned for seven days. Then the sons carried Jacob's body to the cave and laid him to rest with his forefathers and they all returned together to Egypt.

When the realization of their father's death had finally sunk in, the ten brothers began to worry that now that the old man was gone, Joseph might feel free to pay them back for the horrible deed they had done to him years ago. They couldn't be sure that he didn't still hold a grudge against them, so they sent this message to him:

"Our father left these instructions before he died. He said, 'This is what you are to say to Joseph. Tell him I ask him to forgive his brothers for what they did to him.' "

Was this message true or was it contrived for their own protection? We can only guess.

When Joseph received the message, he again cried and his brothers came and fell down in front of him and said, "We will be your slaves."

But Joseph, through his tears, said, "Don't be afraid. Yes, you intended me harm, but God intended it all for good. He put me in the position to save many lives. Don't be afraid. I will always take care of you and your children."

They all continued to live in Egypt and Joseph survived to be a hundred and ten years old and to see his great-great grandchildren. But his time came to live with his fathers and he called his brothers together and made them take an oath to "carry my bones up out of this place."

They took the oath and he died and was embalmed and they placed his body in a coffin in Egypt.

Hero? Certainly to many. Outlaw? Not even to his brothers who wanted to see him dead, but not a saint either. He showed his passion for revenge and then his compassion by weeping openly and often. He was powerful and sometimes arrogant and not always as charitable as the opportunities afforded him. He was forgiving but not always as quickly as he could have been. He was a loving son, a loving brother, and a loving father. He was a good man who fought his demons on a daily basis but trusted God in the long run. I think I see a little bit of him in all of us, and all of us in him.

 # GIDEON

Judges 6–8

The people of Israel were God's chosen people, but they were constantly falling out with Him. They would be under His protection and care for years and then they'd go off in radical directions and fall out of favor for years and then back and forth. At this particular point in Old Testament history, they were on the outs. They were worshiping pagan gods and, in general, doing all manner of evil and God was not happy with them.

They were under the power of the Midianites and were completely overrun by them. The Israelites would plant and then come time for the harvest, the Midianites and others would rush in and grab all they wanted and the Israelites would literally run for the hills and hide in caves. They had no way of protecting themselves and they were being invaded by outsiders who were taking over their land and all they owned. They, like us all, in desperation, turned to the ultimate help when in trouble; they prayed to God. And, like us all, God heard them and acted accordingly.

God sent down a prophet, unnamed and unexplained,

who said, "This is what the Lord God of Israel says: I brought you out of Egypt; out of slavery. I gave you the land of your enemies and then all I asked was that you recognize Me as your one and only God. Told you not to worship any other gods. And have you listened? Not at all."

This would be enough to put a scare into any bunch of people, but God didn't stop with just this message. To show Israel how much He loved them, He took action and this is what He did.

An angel came to the town of Ophrah and sat down under an oak tree that belonged to a man named Joash. Nearby, Joash's son Gideon was threshing wheat in a winepress. Now this last sentence may take a little explaining for those of you who didn't grow up on a farm or in a vineyard.

A winepress was a large, stone vat with a drain hole near the bottom. Overhead, attached to a beam, was usually a rope. Grapes were poured into the vat and a man or woman would get into it and hold on to the rope and stomp the grapes until they were liquid. (Except for the rope, we've all seen Lucy do it hundreds of times.)

Threshing is separating the grain or the seed from the plant or the stalk and the most common way was to beat it. (Thus the expression of "getting a good threshing" when describing an old-fashioned spanking.)

So now we have the picture. And the obvious question is, "Why was Gideon standing in the stone winepress threshing wheat?" And the simple answer is, "He was hiding." He, like all his fellow countrymen, was trying to keep secret anything he had that might be stolen by the Midianites and others who were on the prowl to take advantage of the helpless Jews. But things were about to change.

"The Lord is with you, you mighty man of valor," said this strange angel to Gideon.

And let's take a second on this greeting. Three things could be meant by what this angel said to Gideon. Number one, Gideon could have been a mighty warrior earlier in life that we don't know about. Number two, this might have been prophetic of what was to come, or number three, this angel had a wonderful sense of humor. He was, after all, addressing a man who was hiding in a winepress, beating out wheat stalks so no one would see him. Valor? Bravery? We'll see.

"The Lord is with you, you mighty man of valor," said this strange angel to Gideon.

Gideon looked up at him and said, "If the Lord is with us, why is all this happening to us? Our fathers for generations have told us all the wonderful things God has done for our people, but I don't see it. It looks to me like He's abandoned us. Turned His back on us and here we are under the rule of Midian. I don't get it."

The Lord spoke to Gideon, because the angel was the Lord, and said, "I'm going to send you out to save Israel from Midian.

"Me, Lord?" asked Gideon. He was already addressing him as Lord as he felt deeply that it was God himself to whom he was talking.

"How can I save Israel? My clan is the weakest clan in Manasseh and I'm the least one of my family. I can't save anything."

And God said, "I'll be with you and we'll strike down the Midianites together."

What a team! Anytime God is the other half of your team, you're in the end zone before you start. And Gideon had not only been hand-chosen, he had been promised victory. But that wasn't quite enough for this still-startled young man. He was a little dubious of the whole situation and decided to speak his mind before he went any further. "Lord, if I have found favor in your eyes, give me a sign that this is really you I'm talking to. Really. I'm serious. Don't go away till I come back. I'm going to get an offering and I'm going to set it in front of you, okay? And then you give me some sort of sign that this is really you. Will you wait till I come back?"

"I'll wait till you come back," said the Lord.

Gideon rushed off and killed a goat. He took over a half a bushel of flour and made bread without yeast. He put the meat and the bread in a basket along with broth and brought it back out to where the God/angel was waiting, still under the oak tree.

God said, "Take the meat and the bread and set them on that rock over there. Then pour the broth over them."

Gideon did all this just as he was told, then stepped back to see what was going to happen next.

The angel reached out the staff in his hand and touched the tip of it to the meat and the bread and in an instant a fire flared up and both the goat meat and unleavened bread were consumed in the flames. And in the next instant, the angel disappeared.

Gideon, this mighty man of valor, stood with his mouth gaped open and his eyes frozen on the spot where just seconds ago an angel stood. And at that moment he realized he had truly seen an angel of the Lord. He cried out, "O Lord, I have just seen the angel of God face to face."

A voice, from where he couldn't tell, said, "Be at peace. Don't be afraid. You're not going to die."

This consolation was important, as it was believed anyone who looked on the face of God would surely be put to death. God himself had told Moses this many years before. Now God was assuring Gideon he would be spared for He had things for him to do. He had things in God's name to do.

Gideon was so moved by this encounter that he built an altar to the Lord on that very spot and called it "The Lord Is Peace." This action was from a man who, until the visit from this God/angel, was a worshiper, along with his city and family, of the idol Baal.

God sometimes calls the most unlikely to do the most unlikely.

GIDEON II

That same night as the visit from the angel, God spoke to Gideon again and this time he had some direct and explicit orders.

"Gideon, I want you to take the number two bull from your father's herd, the one that is seven years old, harness him up and tear down your father's Asherah pole and the altar he has built there for Baal."

Why the number two bull? Maybe this was God's way of showing that he was there to help their spiritual lives and not to destroy their economical way of life. The number one bull was spared and still available for its duties, but he definitely had old number two's fate planned. And the Asherah pole? This was a sort of totem pole in honor of a goddess associated with Baal. God was set on wiping out the whole Baal group.

"Now after you've torn down these altars with the bull," God continued, "build a new altar to God on top of the sight. Take the wood from the Asherah pole, chop it up and start a fire and offer the bull up as a burnt offering."

So Gideon gathered up ten of his servants and did exactly what the Lord ordered him to do. The only touch he added of his own was that he did it all after dark. He was afraid of his family and the men of the town and didn't want them to know who was responsible for all of that destruction.

The next morning, the town awoke to the smoldering and stink of burnt wood and burnt bull. Baal's altar was gone. The Asherah pole was in ashes. And the townsfolk were beside themselves.

"Who did this?" they demanded, but no one spoke up. Unfazed by the silence of the guilty, they proceeded with their own investigation and finally came up with a name. Gideon, son of Joash. All signs pointed to him.

They went en masse to Joash's house and demanded he bring his son out and surrender him. "He tore down Baal's altars. He's going to die so you might as well bring him out here right now."

But Joash stood his ground. Not in defiance of Baal and not in defense of God, but for his son, as any real father might do. He looked the crowd in the eye and said, "Are you here to plead Baal's cause? Whoever fights for Baal will be dead by morning. If Baal is a real god, he can defend himself when someone tears down his altar."

And from that day, Gideon was known in his town by the name of Jerubbaal, which means, "let Baal contend."

And here is an irony to contend with. God had handed down the law years before to the Israelites that anyone worshiping idols should be killed. And now one of their own had destroyed an idol and they were out to kill him.

God had found a new warrior and he was ready for battle.

All the Midianites, joined with other forces and enemies of Gideon's people, crossed over the Jordan River and camped in the Valley of Jezreel. They had come to take up arms and make Gideon pay for his sins against their god, Baal. But Gideon had the God of Israel on his side and the spirit of the Lord came over him and he blew a trumpet calling all his people together. He sent out messengers, telling everyone to take up arms and join him. And join him they did, by the thousands.

Gideon, who was by now on very good speaking terms with God, said, "Lord, if you are going to save Israel using me as your instrument, I need a sign. I'll place a wool fleece, a piece of wool material, on the ground. If there is dew only on the fleece in the morning and the ground around it is dry, then I'll know that you will save Israel by my hand."

How many of us have had a similar conversation with God, seeking some sort of sign or approval? Probably all of us.

So that night he placed the piece of wool material on the ground and the next morning he got up and went out and picked up the fleece and squeezed a bowlful of water out of it. But Gideon was not a confident man.

He said, "Lord, now don't be mad at me, but let me ask for one more sign. I'll lay the fleece back out again tonight, but this time let the fleece be dry and let the ground around it be wet."

That night he went through the same routine with the piece of wool material and early the next morning he went out to check it. And sure enough, the fleece was dry and the ground was wet.

God had patiently endured his doubts and reassured him.

He was truly ready for battle now and certain that God was with him and would see him through this ordeal to the end.

Early the next morning Gideon and all his thousands of soldiers set camp at the Spring of Harod. The Lord spoke to him. "Gideon, you have too many men in your army. If you go into battle with all of these troops, Israel will boast that they won the war by their own strength and not by My strength. And it will be hard to prove that kind of thinking wrong. You have to send most of them home."

Gideon, willing to do as God ordered, was a little puzzled as to how he should weed out the ones who should leave from the ones who should stay.

"Announce to them," God said, "that anyone who is afraid can go home right now."

Gideon passed on this order to his army and 22,000 men left and went back to the safety of their homes. Ten thousand stayed to fight.

"Gideon," the Lord said, "there are still too many men. Take them down to the water and I'll sort through them for you. I'll tell you which ones should go and which ones can stay."

So Gideon took 10,000 soldiers down to the river and gave them the "at rest" command and told them to get a drink of water while God decided, unbeknownst to them, on their individual fates.

"Gideon," the Lord said again, "watch them closely. Separate the ones who lap water like a dog from the ones who kneel down to drink."

Only 300 filled their hands with water and lapped it with their tongues like dogs. The other 9,700 knelt down and put their faces in the water to drink. The 9,700 were careless and not watchful. The 300 were careful men, always on the lookout with their heads up and ready for danger.

"Take these three hundred who drink like dogs," God said, "and make them your army and I'll deliver your enemies to you. Send the rest on their way."

The 300 took over the provisions and the trumpets of the others and headed out for the front lines. Young Gideon finally had him an army, for what it was, and a promise from God. He needed nothing more.

God was the spiritual and vocal general of Gideon's army. He gave the orders and Gideon followed them and the next set of orders came in the middle of the night.

"Get up, Gideon, and go down to the Midian camp. If you're afraid to attack, sneak down there with your servant, Purah, and listen to what they're saying to one another. After you eavesdrop and hear what they're saying, you'll feel more encouraged to attack." God knew Gideon needed some reinforcing.

So he took Purah and sneaked down to the outskirts of the huge enemy camp. Just as they arrived they heard one man telling another about a dream he had recently had.

"I dreamed a loaf of bread came tumbling into our camp and struck the tent with such force that the tent collapsed and fell flat on the ground."

"That can mean only one thing," said the other man. "That means that Gideon, the son of Josah, is going to take over our camp. The God of Israel is on his side and we don't have a chance."

This is what Gideon needed to hear. He needed that boost. That surge of confidence. And God knew he did. He thanked God for the information he had gathered and returned to camp, a new and fired-up man.

"Get up!" he yelled to his soldiers. "The Lord is about to give us the Midianites.

He divided up his three hundred into three separate companies and gave them each trumpets and jars with torches inside.

"Follow my lead, men. When we get down to the edge of their camp, surround it and do what I do. When I blow my trumpet, all of you blow your trumpets and then shout 'A sword for the Lord and for Gideon!' "

The troops encircled the camp of Midian and waited for the changing of the guard and then at the most vulnerable and opportune time, they blew their trumpets, broke their jars and flamed their torches and shouted to the top of their voices, "A sword for the Lord and for Gideon." And Midianites and their allies ran from tents and camp, into the night in fear and confusion.

The countryside was a scene of turmoil as other Israelites from all around joined the chase of the Midianites. Two enemy officers, Oreb and Zeeb, were captured and killed and their heads were brought to Gideon who was waiting on the banks of the Jordan.

Gideon was an obedient servant of God and a hero to the men in his charge, but he still had some trouble coming his way from his own people.

GIDEON III

After the initial midnight attack with the three hundred warriors God had hand picked, other tribes were called in to round up, hold, and execute the enemies. Neighboring Israelites from Ephraim, Asher, Naphtali, and Manasseh got in on the act and did their fair share in wiping out a major portion of Midianites. It was the Ephraimites who delivered the heads of Prince Oreb and Prince Zeeb to Gideon. And they were very unhappy about it. Not unhappy to be called on to help, but very upset that they had not been called on sooner. They didn't see enough action and didn't feel important enough in the battle and they let Gideon know exactly what they were feeling.

But smooth-talking Gideon handled them like warm butter. He said, "But look at what you've done even though you were called on late in the game. God allowed you to deliver the two big shots, Oreb and Zeeb. What have I done in comparison to this? You are the men of the hour and everyone knows it."

There was a lot of "aw shucking" and kicking the sand and the Ephraimites wandered off feeling that Gideon was a pretty good fellow after all.

Things were just heating up for Gideon. He and his three hundred were exhausted and weary but they still had a big job to do. They were in hot pursuit of the two king-pins, the two biggies, the two bosses. Their names were King Zebah and King Zalmunna. And Gideon knew that when he caught them, the war would be over.

The chase took him through every town and small village in the region. When he came to Succoth, they stopped and he commanded the townsfolk, "Give my troops bread and water. They're worn out. We'll rest a few minutes and then we're pushing on to find Zebah and Zalmunna."

But the folks of Succoth were scared. They asked, "Do you already have the two kings captured?" And when they were told the two kings were not yet in custody, they refused to help Gideon's army. They were frightened that he would not be successful in capturing the kings and then they would feel the wrath of Zebah and Zalmunna in the future.

This didn't set well with Gideon. He said to the men of the town, "For this attitude toward me and my army, I promise you that after the Lord delivers these two Midian kings into my hands, I will come back here and rip and flail your flesh with thorns and briers."

And they left Succoth in the dust and went to the next town of Penuel and asked for the same favors and were turned down in the same manner. And worn-out ole Gideon reacted in the same manner. "I'll come back through here one day, and when I do, I'll tear down your city tower." (Many towns had towers on the wall of the city that were used for a lookout for attacks from their enemies. These towers were a very essential item of defense.)

The kings Zebah and Zalmunna were on the run with an army of 15,000 up near a little place called Karkor. Gideon and his small band came up the back way and surprised them and even though the two royal leaders ran like villains at the end of a B-western movie, our hero, Gideon himself, chased them down and arrested them.

Not one to forget a promise, Gideon took the same route back home he had taken earlier when hunting for his two prisoners. He marched through Penuel with Zebah and Zalmunna in custody for all to see and paused just long enough to tear down their tower and kill all the men of the city.

He found a young man on the road from Succoth and had him write down all the names of the officials of that city, 77 in all, and then paraded the kings into town and said to the 77, "Do you remember me? Remember my men? They're the ones you wouldn't give bread and water to when they were falling over from exhaustion. You merely taunted them and never thought they would have the kings of Midian in chains. Well, look again, gentlemen and meet Zebah and Zalmunna."

And then he took the 77 elders of the town out and ripped and flailed their flesh with thorns and briers.

You can't say Gideon was not a man of his word.

The trial and execution of Zebah and Zalmunna were simple. Gideon put the first and only question to them, "Who were the men you killed at the battle of Tabor?"

"Men like you," they replied with no remorse nor evident fear. "They carried themselves like a prince would. Yes, they were very much like you in many ways."

"That's because those were my brothers," judge Gideon said. "They were the sons of my mother and if you had spared their lives then, I would spare yours now."

This is the first hint we have that there were personal feelings involved between these three men. We hadn't previously known about Gideon's brothers or about his vendetta. But his next move shows us without doubt that this has become a family thing. He turns to his eldest son, Jether, and passes final sentence by commanding him, "Kill them."

This is a kindness to Jether in allowing him an important and historical hand in the execution of kings and at the same time a dishonor to the kings by showing them that they aren't important enough for Gideon, himself, to raise his hand to them.

But Jether spoils the moment. He refuses to pull his sword. Whether out of fear or out of youthful inexperience, we don't know. But the kings, who we have noted before, showed no fear in the face of death, used their final moments on earth to try to insult their accuser. They jeered, "Come on, Gideon. Do it yourself. Be a man."

And Gideon was a man and he did it. He stepped up

and killed King Zebah and King Zalmunna by his own hand. Then he took the ornaments, the jewelry, off their camels' necks as a sign of personal victory over the enemy.

GIDEON IV

All Israel came to Gideon and begged him, "Rule over us. Be our king. Then your son after you will be our king and your grandson after him. We need you because you saved us from Midian."

"No," Gideon refused, "I'll not rule over you and neither will my son. But God will rule over you. God will be your king. But there is one thing I would like for you to do for me."

The people couldn't wait to serve him in any way he wanted. "What can we do for you, Gideon?"

"Each of you, give me one gold earring that you plundered from the Midianites."

The people gladly spread a robe on the ground and each man walked by and laid their piece of jewelry on the pile and when the robe was gathered up, there were 43 pounds of gold, not counting the pendants and ornamental camel collars and purple garments belonging to the Midian kings. Gideon took all the gold, none for himself, and made it into an ephod which was a sacred vest-like piece of clothing, trimmed in gold and beautiful jewels and worn by the high priest. It was very royal, very rich.

He had this ephod made to commemorate their victory over Midian and placed it in his hometown of Ophrah. But its effect differed from its intent. All Israel traveled to see it and its beauty and it became an object of worship. It was held in too high esteem and its purpose as a reminder of what God had done for Israel was lost. It became an idol just as Baal was an idol and it proved to be bad for Gideon and his family and his people.

Midian never raised its oppressive head to Israel again. All during the rest of Gideon's life, for the next 40 years, Israel was at peace.

Gideon went home to live and raise his family/families. He had many wives and concubines and was the father of 71 sons. The Good Book tells us Gideon died at a good old age and was buried in the tomb of his father in Ophrah.

But no sooner had they laid his body to rest, Israel turned again to Baal. They forgot all about God and everything he had done for them. They forgot about the battle with the 300 men. Forgot about how life was before God and Gideon took over. About how the Midianites would raid their harvest and how they had prayed to heaven for help. They forgot how hungry and helpless they once were and forgot who had stepped up and faced their enemies for them.

And they forgot the family he left behind. Gideon's wives and sons were shown no respect and no kindness for all Gideon had done for his people in the name of God.

Gideon: The reluctant hero. The weak hero. The frightened hero.

He was a mighty man of valor after all. He may have hidden at one time and he may have needed a little encouragement and he may have needed to be bolstered and reassured once or twice, but let's give him a break. After all, he was only human.

 # SAMSON

Judges 13–16

Samson was the Superman of the Old Testament. He was a folk-hero, a circus strongman, a legend, a super-hero. He was Hercules. He was Atlas. He was a little baby born in Canaan about 1,000 years before Christ.

You can find his story in the Book of Judges. As a matter of fact, he was known as a judge. But there is really no record of him ever sitting in judgment of anyone or anything. He wasn't even much of a religious leader. What he was, was . . . a lover. And that was his strength, (no pun intended) and also his weakness.

His story and his life started out rather miraculously. An angel came to his mother, who had no children and thought herself barren, and said, "You're going to have a son, but here's the deal. While you're pregnant don't drink any wine of any kind and don't eat any unclean food." Un-clean food included rabbits, pigs, camels, shellfish, eagles, owls, ravens, and hawks. Not a bad rule to go by today un-less you get a late-night craving for pork barbeque or clams as some pregnant women do.

The angel continued, "And after your son is born, you are never to cut his hair. He will be a Nazarite and his mission in life will be to begin the deliverance of Israel out of the hands of the Philistines."

A little explanation about that last sentence: The Philistines, for 40 years, had been ruling over Israel because God was punishing the Jews for their sins. And Samson was to be the man who was to put a stop to all this or at least start the ball rolling to stop all this.

Now the angel said he was to be a Nazarite, not to be confused with a Nazarene, one from Nazareth. The Nazarite is best explained as a sort of religious sect, sort of a monk. Not one removed from society like a monk, but one vowed to be different and still be among society. Think of our Amish. The Nazarite was special and there were two different types. The temporary and the perpetual. The temporary was one who took a vow for maybe a month at a time like we do Lent or a New Year's resolution. The New Year's resolution is lucky to last a month. But the perpetual Nazarite was from birth and on demand from God. And there were three main things he couldn't do.

He could not drink wine of any kind or even use vinegar or even eat grapes or raisins. He could never cut his hair. He could never go near a dead body. The Lord said even if his father or his mother or his sister or his brother dies, he could have no contact with the body or go near it. If someone should even die suddenly in his presence, he would have to shave his head and start the cleansing process all over. And there's an elaborate ritual spelled out for them in this case.

These were purifications and disciplines that God stressed for those who chose or were chosen for this different way of life. Back to the Amish, they have certain things that set them apart from the rest of the world. They have to wear a beard after they marry. They have to dress in a certain way. The women dress simply and wear bonnets and prayer caps.

The Hassidic Jews are set apart with their hats and braids down the sides of their faces. Like them, Samson was a vegetable in a box of candy. And "different" is not an easy lifestyle to live up to.

But back to the angel and Samson's mother. After this brief meeting, the angel left and the mother ran immediately to tell her husband what had just happened. You must realize that she didn't *know* at this time that she had been talking to an angel but she had some sense that he was some sort of "man of God." She told her husband, "I didn't ask him his name or ask him where he came from but he told me we are going to have a child and he's going to be a Nazarite" and on and on.

The husband, Manoah, needed more info. He couldn't go on just what little his wife had told him so he prayed to God for the stranger to come again. He said, "Lord, we don't know how to raise a Nazarite. We've got lots of questions so please send him back and tell us how to raise this boy he said is coming to us."

So the angel came again. To the wife again. And she told him, "Wait right here while I go and get my husband," and she took off and found Manoah and told him to "come a-runnin'. The angel is back."

Manoah jumped up and ran with her out to the field and there stood the stranger. Manoah said, "Are you the one who talked to my wife?"

The stranger/angel said, "Yeah, I'm the one."

Manoah said, "Well, what're the rules? How do we raise the boy?"

And the stranger/angel said, "Just do exactly what I told your wife to do. She can't drink wine or eat unclean food." And that's all the instruction he would give. No rules on rearing the child. Just the command to do as he had already told them to do and he didn't repeat it. And Manoah, being a gentle man, didn't push it. Instead he said, "We'd like for you to stay for supper. We'll roast a goat for you."

The stranger/angel said, "I'll stay but I won't eat. But if you're going to prepare something, prepare a burnt offering and offer it to the Lord."

Manoah looked at him and bit his lip a little and was starting to get a little suspicious as to whether he was being put on or not. He looked this mysterious stranger right in the eye and said, "What's your name?"

The stranger said, "Why do you want to know my name? Trust me, it's beyond your understanding."

So Manoah cooked a goat and offered it as a sacrifice. And an amazing thing happened. As the flames from the fire of the altar shot up toward the sky, the stranger, the angel of the Lord, ascended in the flames and disappeared into the heavens. And then Manoah and his wife knew for sure who this stranger had been. And they were scared nearly to death. They fell down on the ground on their faces and Manoah cried, "I know we're going to die because we have just seen God."

But his wife said, "No, no, Manoah. Listen. If God had meant to kill us, He wouldn't have accepted our offering or told us all these things he wants us to do."

And she was right. The little woman, whom Manoah didn't trust to get all the information correct with the angel on the first visit, was now the voice of reason and good sense. And this same woman was the future mother of one of the most colorful characters to ever grace the pages of the Holy Scriptures. And she was to name him Samson, which means "little sun." And he would grow and be blessed and it would be said that the spirit of the Lord would stir inside him.

SAMSON II

The Philistines were a pagan nation of people. They had inhabited Palestine and were at odds with the Jews, sometimes violently and sometimes just annoyingly. And sometimes they were downright friendly as we are about to see. But before we see, and look in on Samson as an adult, let me warn you about him. Samson, although born under rather miraculous circumstances and having the spirit of the Lord stirring in him, was not always a perfect example of a man of God, as *we* aren't always. And this simply may have just been a part of his mission as I feel was a part of David's. This was God's way of letting us know that He loves us and tolerates us and forgives us even though we aren't perfect in body, mind, and spirit.

Now Samson was a womanizer from the word go. The next time we find anything about him at all in the Bible, he's a grown man and has traveled down to the town of Timnath, about four miles from where he lived. He saw a young Philistine woman down there who caught his eye, turned his head, and generally turned him on. So he went back home and told his mother and father, "I saw this Philistine woman today I want. Go down there and get her for me. I want to marry her."

Now it was the custom of the day for parents to arrange the marriages of their children, so this wasn't such an outlandish request, except that she was a Philistine and he was a Jew. So his mamma and daddy said, "Samson, honey, isn't there anyone among our people you could marry? Couldn't you marry one of your own kind? A nice Jewish girl?"

Samson's simple reply to this consideration was, "Get her for me."

And although this may sound harsh and disrespectful to his parents, we are told this decision was of God, because God was about to use this situation to start pitting Samson against the Philistines.

So he and his mother and father took off and headed down to Timnath and while they were traveling down there, a lion attacked them. Actually, it attacked Samson, because someway or another his parents never knew anything about it. But when the lion jumped out at him (maybe they were walking ahead of him planning the upcoming wedding), Samson grabbed him and tore him apart barehanded. Killed him right there on the spot and left him lying. And then continued on down the road and never said a word to his mamma or daddy about it.

They all three went into town to meet this girl he had fallen for, apparently arranged for the marriage, and then went on back home. Because we're told that they went back later for the wedding and while they were traveling to Timnath the second time, Samson detoured a little and looked for the carcass of the lion that he had killed on the last trip. And sure enough he found it lying over in the weeds and in the lion's body a swarm of bees were flying around and they had made honey in the lion's carcass and Samson reached in and got a couple of handfuls and ate some as he walked along. And when he caught up with mom and dad, he gave them some, too. And they all three went walking down the road eating honey. But he still didn't tell them where he got it or anything at all about killing the lion.

They had the wedding and a seven-day wedding feast as was customary. You think you've been to a wedding, how about a seven-day wedding reception?

On the first day of the feast, Samson met 30 men who were kin and friends of the bride. And Samson, who was a fun-loving, teasing kind of guy, said to these 30 men, "Let's play a little game. I'll give you a riddle and if you can answer it, I'll give you 30 linen garments and 30 sets of clothes."

He came up with this gamble out of the blue. (This whole story reminds me so much of my daddy who would just sit around and think of things to bet on. Any game or any challenge to put to people and make them squirm would entertain him.)

So these 30 guys said, "Okay, give us the riddle."

And Samson said:

"Out of the eater came something to eat
Out of the strong came something sweet."

For three days they worked on this riddle and could not come up with the answer. Finally, they went to Samson's wife and said, "Get your husband to tell you the answer to that riddle or we're going to burn your father's house to the ground."

These boys took bar bets seriously. They had no intention of losing to some Jew who had come to town throwing his weight around.

So the wife went crying to Samson and said, "You have given my people a riddle and you haven't even told *me* the answer. It's not fair. I'm your wife. If you loved me you'd tell me."

Samson grinned and said, "I haven't even told my mother

and father the answer. Why do you think I would tell you?"

So she cried for the rest of the seven-day feast. Cried the whole time and whined, until on the seventh day he finally broke down and told her the answer. Dried her tears right up. She sneaked off and told her people what she had found out and they came and found Samson and said, "We've got the answer. You asked the riddle:

> 'Out of the eater came something to eat
> Out of the strong came something sweet.'

"And the answer is: What is sweeter than honey? What is stronger than a lion?"

You see they answered it with a question and that's how "Jeopardy" was born.

Samson was in a rage. He said a rather strange thing right here. He said, "If you had not plowed with my heifer, you would not have found out my riddle."

He was accusing them of coercing his wife; coaxing her; bargaining with her. Some interpret it to mean he was accusing them of having sex with her. This is how she extracted it from Samson, as would other women in time, and one tends to judge others by one's self. But this judge was mad and dangerous and embarrassed and not to be reasoned with at the time. And on top of everything else he had a gambling debt to pay. He had just lost the game and he knew his wife had betrayed him, maybe even slept with the enemy, and he knew he owed 30 guys 30 pieces of linen and 30 sets of clothes. And where was he going to get them?

Simple. Samson went down to Ashkelon, a little town down the road, killed 30 men, stripped their clothes off them and brought the clothes back and gave them to the 30 guys who won the bet. And while everyone was in a giving mood, his wife was given to his best man. And *that* wedding feast was over.

The Bible actually says "the spirit of the Lord came mightily upon him and he went down to Ashkelon and killed 30 men." The Lord empowered him and directed him to do this. Why? The only possible explanation is that his mission was to destroy the Philistines, wipe out as many as possible, and this, in his small way, was a beginning.

Later on in the fall, around harvest time, Samson decided he wanted to go back to Timnath and see his "wife." He was getting a little lonesome, feeling a little bad about what all had happened, so he went bearing gifts. Actually one gift. A kid. A young goat. Samson was a romantic devil.

This was his peace offering and he used it to try to get in to see her. Now we have been told that "his wife was given to his best man" but it doesn't make it clear who gave her to the best man. At first reading, and considering his state of mind, we tend to think it was Samson himself. But here we find out exactly who the giver was. As Samson starts to enter his "wife's" room, her father steps in front of him and says, "Hold it. You're not going in there. I was so sure that you hated her that I gave her to your best man. But I tell you what. She's got a younger sister who is really better looking than she is. Why don't you take her?"

Samson was not happy. Again he went into a rage. He said, "This time I know I'm justified in whatever I do to the Philistines. And I'm going to do it up right this time."

And here we find that Samson is not only a little bit mean, as we have already thought, but that he is also extremely creative. He goes out and catches three hundred foxes, which is no small feat, and ties their tails together, which is an even less small feat. Then he ties torches between each pair of tails, lights the torches and turns them loose in the Philistines' grain fields, olive groves, and vineyards. That set fire to everything they had growing — not to mention what it must have done to the foxes.

When the Philistines came out and saw what had happened they said, "Who did this?" And they were told it was Samson. And they were told he had done it because his father-in-law had given his wife to his best man. (And you think the storyline on *The Young And The Restless* is unbelievable!)

Well, the Philistines were not without their anger and creativity, so they set out to find Samson's wife and her father. And when they found them, they set both of them on fire. Burned them to death.

And Samson went wild. He vowed his revenge and tore into them immediately and viciously and killed we don't-know-how-many right there on the spot. And then he retreated down to Etam to rest. He found himself a small cave and he lay low for a while because he knew the whole Philistine nation would be looking for him.

Samson III

The Philistines went up to Judah, up in Samson's territory, with their armies. And the men of Judah came out to meet them and asked, "Why have you come up here, to fight us?"

The Philistines said, "No. We've come to get Samson. To do to him what he did to our people."

So at this point, 3,000 men from Judah, Samson's own people, went out looking for him and found him in the cave. They said, "What's wrong with you? Do you know what you're doing to us? Don't you realize that the Philistines are rulers over us and you're acting like this toward them?"

Samson, in all his self-righteousness, said, "I merely did to them what they did to me."

And the 3,000 said, "Well, we've come to tie you up and turn you in to the Philistine army."

Samson said, "Okay, but promise me you won't kill me. Promise me you'll only tie me up."

They said, "No, we won't kill you."

You see Samson had a plan. He let them tie him up with two new ropes and march him down through the rocks from the cave like a prisoner going to the gallows. And when the Philistines saw them coming, they came running toward him hollering and shouting and ready for blood.

And the Scriptures tell us, and I quote, "The spirit of the Lord came mightily upon him," and he snapped the ropes in shreds and they just melted off his hands.

Samson looked down on the ground in the dust and just like in those old western movies where you always saw cattle skulls lying around, he saw the skeletal pieces of a donkey and reached down and picked up the jawbone and started swinging it as his only weapon. And he killed 1,000 men. And when he was through he gave a war cry. He yelled, "With the jawbone of an ass, I have slain a thousand men."

Then he slung the jawbone in the air as a sign that the battle was over. And the first sensation he felt as he stood there after this miraculous feat of one against a thousand, the first sensation he felt was that he was . . . thirsty.

And he cried out to God, "You have given me this victory. Now are you going to let me die of thirst at the hands of my enemies?"

Impatient. Crude. Selfish. Mean. Vicious. Brutal. But a man of God. Because at that very moment God opened up a hole in the ground and sweet, cold water came spurting out of it. A spring right there in the middle of the desert. And Samson drank it up until his strength returned. And for the next 20 years he led Israel in the face of the ruling Philistines.

Samson IV

Now the next time we look in on Samson, this man of God, this man whose birth was announced by an angel of the Lord, this man who was born to lead his people and who, we're told, felt the spirit stir within and come upon him at inspired and important times in his life, the next time we look in on him, he's visiting a house of prostitution on the Gaza Strip.

And the word gets around Gaza really quick. The people of the town whisper, "Samson is here. Let's surround the house he's gone in, wait for him and kill him when he comes out."

Samson's attitude, actions, position, and strength have made him a right despised character there in the area. And except for his own people, not many others care for him.

So they have him surrounded and are waiting for him at the gate of the city. They figure he'll be in there all night so their plan is to kill him at dawn when he comes out. But Samson comes out a little earlier than expected and with a little more gusto than expected. He comes out at midnight, which catches them off guard, and he comes out in a whirlwind.

Apparently he has some hint he might be in danger because he comes out of the house, grabs the gates of the city and tears them out of the ground along with the two posts that anchor them, and puts them on his shoulders and carries them to the top of the hill that overlooks the city.

Now would you want to be on the front lines that attack a man who is carrying the city gates with him as he leaves town? Nobody does and nobody did.

SAMSON V

Sometime later Samson got himself a real girlfriend. As we have mentioned, Samson had a weakness for women, but he really fell for this one and her name was Delilah. And when the Philistines found out about this relationship, they agreed that this just might be a good way to get to Samson. So a few of them went to Delilah and said if you will help us find the secret to his strength, we'll each give you 1,100 pieces of silver. Translated, this is 1,100 shekels. A shekel then was a day's pay worth somewhere around 65 cents. So figure 1,100 shekels at 65 cents would be about $715. And multiply that by some or a few or many, because we aren't told how many Philistine rulers came to her but we know they were plural and they each promised $715, so Delilah was getting into some pretty good blood money. Not a cheap bounty.

Delilah thought the thing over and came up with a plan of her own. First she came right out and asked him, "What makes you so strong and what will make you weak?"

And Samson looked her right in the eye and said, "Honey, I'll level with you. If you tie me up with seven fresh withs (a with was the cord they made into bowstrings), I'll become as weak as any other man."

Now I don't know exactly what all Samson and Delilah were into, but she called the Philistines into her bedroom that night and told them to hide and then she coyly tied old Samson up with the bowstrings and stepped back and yelled, "Samson, the Philistines are here."

And he jumped up and broke those bowstrings like they were threads. And the Philistines just watched in silence and awe and stayed hid because they still didn't know what made him strong. She tried again, Delilah did. She told him later, "You know you made a fool out of me. We're close. We're lovers. Tell me the secret of your strength. The mystery of those big strong muscles."

Samson, being the "ole boy" he was, looked her in the eye and said, "Okay, honey, I'll level with you. Tie me up with new ropes that have never been used and I'll become as weak as a lamb. Like putty in your hands or at least as weak as any other man."

Now we begin to see a pattern to Samson here. First off, this is not the first time his enemies have used a woman to get to him. Remember his wife and the riddle? She cried and whined for days before he finally gave in and told her what she wanted to know. And this new rope thing. He had used that one before when he told his people to tie him up back at the cave in Etam. He knew he could crack out of that one easily enough, so here he was using the same trick again.

And apparently Delilah liked tying him up because she set the whole thing up again. Got the Philistines to hide in the bedroom and then tied him up with new rope. And then she jumped back and yelled, "Samson, the Philistines are here!"

And Samson jumped up and snapped off those ropes like *they* were threads.

Delilah was not a happy girl. She was getting madder by the minute. Samson was acting cute and playing games and she was getting farther away from that money all the time. So she tried again, "Samson, you've been lying to me. You're making a fool of me. Tell me once and for all what is the source of your strength?"

Samson looked at her and thought about it for a minute and finally said, "Honey, I'm gonna level with you. Weave my hair into seven braids. Pull it tight and stick a hairpin in each braid and I'll be as weak as any man can be."

I think Samson liked the pain that came with it.

So Delilah started all over. She called in the Philistines, whom I'm sure were getting pretty tired of this game themselves. She braided his hair and when he was asleep she yelled, "Samson, the Philistines are here!" and in an instant Samson was on his feet and ready to fight.

Delilah was really mad now. She stayed on him everyday. Nagged him. Goaded him. Wore him down to where he just didn't want to hear about it anymore. She finally hit him with the trusty, old standby. She said, "Samson, if you loved me, you'd tell me. What makes you so strong?"

So Samson did. He looked her right in the eye and said, "Honey, I'm gonna level with you." And this time . . . he did. He said, "No razor has ever touched my head. I was given this strength through my hair by God himself. If I ever cut my hair, I would, honestly, be as weak as any other man."

Now every man in the world should take a lesson right here. A woman may not always know to what extent a man is lying to her, but she always knows when he's telling her the truth. And Delilah knew from the look in his eye that he really was leveling with her this time. So she called the Philistines once more and told them to come tonight and hide out in her bedroom and told them when they came this time to bring the money with them because this is it.

And the Philistines came and hid and Samson fell asleep with his head in Delilah's lap. When he was deep asleep, she motioned for a man to come into the room and shave his head. And Samson never woke up. Not until it was all over and Delilah yelled for the last time, "Samson, the Philistines are here!"

But this time when he jumped up, he was helpless. The Philistines came out, grabbed him, gouged his eyes out, put chains on him and took him to prison. And he spent his days in prison grinding at the mill as an ox might do, round and round in circles and in chains and in total darkness for he was blinded for the rest of his life. But one thing happened they didn't count on. Each day his hair grew a little more and a little more.

As time went by, the Philistines had a celebration in honor of the pagan god Dagon, whom they accredited for bringing their enemy Samson into captivity. They were gathered together in their temple celebrating big and singing Dagon's praises and just having them a high ole time, when somebody came up with a really funny idea. Being as how they were celebrating having Samson in custody, why not go get him out of prison, bring him to the temple and have some fun with him. So they did.

They brought Samson to the temple floor and made sport of him. They watched him stumble around in his blindness and laughed at him and patted themselves on the back for having captured him. The wild man in captivity. The caged strongman. The outlaw of Judah, jailed.

The temple was packed with men and women and all the Philistine lords, and on the roof alone, looking down into the arena area where Samson was on display, there were 3,000 thrill-hungry spectators.

We don't know how many thousands of Philistines were squeezed in there that day, but we do know that at one point, whether it was to rest him or to place him in a spot where more people could get a better look at him, they placed Samson between two center pillars. Samson, sensing this, said to the boy who was holding his hand and guiding him around, "Let me lean against the pillars for a minute."

And as Samson reached out and felt a pillar on his right and one on his left, he said a prayer. He said, "God give me my strength just one more time and let me have just one more act of revenge for my two eyes."

And he reached to each center pillar, one to his right, one to his left and made one last plea. He cried, "Let me die with the Philistines!" And he bent his knees and pushed with all the Nazarite power God had given him and the temple crumbled, killing everybody that was in it. And the Scriptures tell us, "He killed more in his death than he ever did in his life."

Blind. Kamikaze. Suicidal. Sacrificial. Finally unselfish. Whatever adjective you choose. He was a man of God.

The last mention of Samson is that his brothers came down and got his body and took him home to be buried. His mission was over. He did what he was born to do. He killed Philistines. And every event in his life, no matter how sordid or how ungodly it may seem to you, was a steppingstone in doing this final act. Everything he did kept pitting him against the enemy until he was finally put in a unique situation where he could get the largest number in one fell swoop.

God works in ways we don't always understand and uses people we may not always approve of. And he may be using you for something you aren't aware of right now or may never be.

Hero or outlaw? He performed God's plan in ways that sometimes made him look suspect and would have gotten him locked up by the standards of the law. With most wonderful old characters in the Bible as with most characters from any walk of life, if you inspect them closely, you'll find a little of the outlaw in their heroics.

# RUTH

The Book of Ruth

The Book of Ruth, as it is usually referred to, is really no book at all. It's a short story among books in the Old Testament. Only four chapters long, it takes place in the early days of Israel when judges ruled, before they had kings.

A very serious famine had hit the land of Judah and a man by the name of Elimelech, who was living in Bethlehem with his wife, Naomi, and their two sons, Mahlon and Kilion, decided his best bet for survival was to go down to Moab and try to make a living there. Moab was a sometimes friendly, sometimes unfriendly neighbor of Judah, so the family agreed that this would be as good a gamble as any.

But as life often does, it jumped up and grabbed Elimelech in the heart when he was least expecting it and he died down in Moab and left Naomi a single mother with two sons to look after. The boys, Mahlon and Kilion, grew up and found two Moabite women they vowed to love and married Orpah and Ruth, respectively.

After ten years of marriage, both Mahlon and Kilion

came to the same end as their father. At a very young age, they died and left young wives behind. And then there were three; three widows living together, Naomi and her two daughters-in-law, Orpah and Ruth.

Word came to Moab that the famine was over up in Judah. God had intervened and there was food and rain and harvest and planting and things were back to normal. Naomi's thoughts were of home, so she gathered up her daughters-in-law and headed back to the land she knew and where she felt at home. But on the road, as she had ample time to think as she traveled, she stopped and turned to Orpah and Ruth and said, "Girls, this is the right thing for me to do but not necessarily the right thing for you. Go back to your homes, to your mothers, where you'll be more comfortable. And may God always show you the greatest kindness that you showed to my sons and to me. And my prayer will always be that you both find another husband deserving of you."

And then she kissed them each and hugged them and they all three began to weep and the girls said, "We are going with you."

"No, no, no," Naomi said. "Go back home. Why would you want to come with me? I'm too old to marry again and certainly too old to have more sons for you to marry. (It was ancient Jewish law that the brother of a deceased man would marry his widowed sister-in-law.) And even if I thought I might, would you wait for my sons to grow up before you married again? I don't think so. No, my daughters, this is hard for you I know, but it's even harder for me. Go home, please, and live your lives. I love you but I can do nothing for you now."

And again they cried together and Orpah kissed her

mother-in-law and told her good-bye and turned and went back toward Moab. But Ruth, when she kissed her, clung to Naomi and wouldn't turn her loose.

"Look at your sister-in-law, Ruth. She's already started her journey home. Go with her," Naomi pleaded. "Go home with her."

But Ruth continued to cling to Naomi's arms and continued to cry. "Don't make me go back. Wherever you go, I'll go. Wherever you stay, I'll stay. Your family and friends will be my family and friends. Your God will be my God. Where you die and are buried, I will die and be buried."

And Naomi finally realized the sincerity of Ruth's passion and she stopped urging her to go home. So together they traveled on home to Bethlehem.

When they arrived, the whole town was surprised and excited to see them. They came out and greeted them and the townsfolk said, "Can this really be Naomi?"

But a certain cynicism had come over Naomi and she proved to be not the same woman she was when she left years ago. She corrected her old friends in a hurry. "Don't call me Naomi." (The word Naomi means "pleasant.") "Call me Mara because God has made my life bitter." (The word Mara means "bitter.") "I went away from here a happy woman, full of life, but the Lord has brought me back empty and sad and afflicted. So don't call me Naomi. I'm nothing but a string of misfortune and tragedy. My husband died. My two sons died. I'm a bitter woman. Call me Mara."

So here she was, back home, alone, except for a foreign daughter-in-law whom everyone was looking askew at because they just didn't have a lot of love for a Moabite girl, and with an attitude that didn't exactly endear her to old friends. Yes, life for Naomi/Mara had changed and she wasn't the least bit happy about it.

It was a custom of the times that those who harvested the fields, be it barley or wheat or what-have-you, would leave behind a little for the poor who would come behind and glean what had fallen on the ground or what was still growing that had not been picked clean. This allowed the needy a little dignity over begging. And even though it was a dangerous job for a lone woman out there in the fields with all the men laborers, Ruth saw it as an opportunity to feed her mother-in-law and herself. She told Naomi what she was going to do and Naomi gave her permission.

She found a random field and fell in behind the pickers and began her long, hot day, gathering barley. The owner of this random field, a man named Boaz, came out in mid-morning to look over his crop and his employees. To all of them he extended the greeting, "The Lord be with you."

And they all greeted him, "The Lord bless you." Pretty good rapport between labor and management.

"Who's the young girl?" Boaz asked his foreman as he was standing looking out over the fields.

"She's that Moabite girl that came up here with Naomi. She begged me to let her glean behind the pickers and she's been working hard since early morning. Only stopped one time for a short break."

Boaz called Ruth over to the side and spoke to her affectionately like a father figure, "Listen to me, my daughter. Don't go off in any other fields and do what you're doing here. It's not safe. Stay here with the servant girls and with my men. I've told them not to touch you, not to harm you. Whenever you get thirsty, you stop and go get a drink. But you be careful and don't try this anywhere else."

Ruth bowed her face down to the ground and said, "Why have I found such favor in your eyes? I'm just a foreign girl. Why have you noticed me so?"

Boaz said, "I know all about you. I know what you've done for your mother-in-law since the death of your husband. I know how you've stuck by her and left your mother and father and came here to live with her. May the Lord reward you for what you have done. You are a brave and good woman."

"I'm honored, my lord," said Ruth. "I hope I always find favor in your eyes. You have spoken so kindly to me even though I am not even equal to your servant girls."

When they broke for lunch, Boaz called her over and gave her bread and wine to dip it in. He offered her roasted grain and she ate all she wanted and had some left over. When they all went back to work, Boaz called his men together and said, "Don't just leave some behind in the ground. Pull out some stalks and leave them loose for her on top of the ground. And don't make fun of her and don't tease her. And don't touch her." And the men went back to work with orders they knew not to ignore.

Ruth worked in the fields until late that evening and after threshing, carried home over a half a bushel of barley. She couldn't wait to show Naomi what she had earned that day and even brought with her the roasted grain left over from lunch.

"Where did you work today?" Naomi asked her.

"I worked for a man by the name of Boaz and he was so nice to me. He took notice of me and protected me and treated me like he really cared."

"Well, bless him," said Naomi with a smile. "That man, Boaz, is our closest relative, Ruth."

"He even told me to stay with his workers until they finished gathering all of his grain," Ruth told her excitedly.

"It's good that he's looking out for you. Be sure to stay with his girls," Naomi warned, "because with them you'll be safe out there in the fields where anything can happen."

So Ruth continued to go to Boaz's fields and stayed close to his servant girls until all the barley and wheat was finished. And all this time she lived with her mother-in-law and took care of her.

Ruth II

Deep in thought and concern for the future of her young daughter-in-law, Naomi said to Ruth one day, "My dear daughter, I should be finding a proper home for you. You can't just live with me the rest of your life. You need a man and a family. I told you that Boaz is our next of kin, so tonight when he is winnowing (blowing off the chaff — separating the impurities) the barley down on the threshing floor, you need to go down there and see him. Take a bath and perfume yourself and put on your best clothes. Sneak in and don't let him know you're there until he's finished working and then finished eating and drinking. When he goes to lie down, give him time to get asleep and then slip in and uncover his feet and lie down and he'll tell you what to do next."

Ruth, ever obedient, said, "I'll do whatever you say."

So she bathed and doused herself in perfume and put on her Sabbath best and went down to the threshing floor where Boaz was working and waited until he had finished work and eaten supper and taken of a few spirits. She watched him lie down by a pile of grain and cover himself with a blanket and when she thought he was fast asleep, she quietly eased over and pulled the blanket up and lay down at his feet and fell asleep herself, there on the floor.

It was sometime in the middle of the night when Boaz rolled over and felt something or someone next to him. He raised up and said, "Who are you?"

"I'm your servant Ruth. Spread your blanket over me since you are my next of kin."

This was a pretty brazen move for a little foreign woman. She was in all reality proposing marriage to this middle-aged rich man. She was coming on to him in the strongest possible way. Neither she nor Boaz could mistake what was being offered here. Boaz certainly had no doubts about it. He said, "Bless you, my daughter. This is a great kindness you show me. And even greater is the kindness that you have chosen me instead of running after some of the younger men in town. You are a woman of great character and I'll do all for you that you ask because I am a near kin of yours. But there is a problem you aren't aware of. I am not the *nearest* kin of yours. There's someone closer kin than I."

Ruth was crushed and confused, but Boaz went on. "Stay here for the night and in the morning if he, your next of kin, wants to take you for his wife, I will walk away. But if he doesn't, then as sure as God lives, I will do it. But lie back down and stay here with me until morning."

So she did. She stayed the night with him there on the floor and come sometime in the early a.m., she got up and left before the dawn light so that no one would see her or recognize her.

As she was slipping out, Boaz stopped her and said softly, "Bring me your shawl and hold it out," and he poured grain in it so she would have food to take home. And then he whispered, "Don't let anyone know that you came to the threshing floor."

Ruth stole away through town in the early morning light to her mother-in-law's house. When she arrived, Naomi asked her, "How did it go?"

Ruth confided everything in Naomi. She told her every detail about the night and how he had gotten up and poured grain in her shawl and said to her, "Don't go back to your mother-in-law empty-handed."

Naomi smiled and said, "All you have to do now is wait, because I assure you this man will not rest until this matter is settled. It will happen today."

Later that same morning, Boaz went up to the town gate and sat down and waited on the man he knew was bound to pass through. The "next of kin." And soon he did and Boaz called to him, "Come over here, friend, and sit down. I want to talk to you."

What Boaz was about to do was in accordance with local law. All law was designed to keep family property in the family so in order for any belongings to be transferred, a public meeting had to be held at the city gates in front of a group of witnesses. The "next of kin" had to be offered the property first and if he refused, the "next of kin" was in line if he wanted it. This was a form of the old Levirate law in Deuteronomy. And this was a gamble Boaz was playing, but one he had to play to get the woman he wanted.

He called ten elders of the city to come sit down with them at the gate and then he began his little speech. "Naomi has come back from Moab and she's selling a piece of land that belonged to our kinfolk, Elimelech. If you are interested in buying it you can do so in the presence of these witnesses. If you are not interested, then I am next in line and I may be interested."

The "next of kin" spoke up immediately, "I'm interested."

"Okay," said Boaz, "when you buy the land you also acquire the dead man's widow. The dead man is Elimelech's son, Mahlon, to whom it was passed down. So you will acquire the young Moab woman with the property."

To further understand the Levirate law is to further understand this touchy situation Boaz was risking. Under the law, if you married a kinsman's widow, any sons she bore you would not legally be yours but would be the legal sons of the dead husband and all properties of the dead husband would then go to the sons. Therefore, if you take a young widow still in her childbearing years, you risk losing everything in the end that you thought you might gain in the beginning.

"Whoa, wait a minute. Then I don't want the property. This might endanger my own estate," the "next of kin" guy said. And endanger his estate it would. All the time he took from furthering his own investments and working his own land and put into working the land acquired through the "Ruth deal" would be lost as soon as a son was born to them as the property would then go in the son's name. No, ole "next of kin" decided right then and there he wanted no part of this deal. And sly old Boaz was glad.

"I don't want the property," said "the next of kin." "You buy it yourself," and he took off his sandal and handed it to Boaz, as this was the custom when property was transferred from one to another.

Boaz stood up and announced to the elders, "You are the witnesses. Today I'm buying all the property from Naomi that belonged to Elimelech and Kilion and Mahlon. I am also acquiring Ruth as my wife."

The elders stood and said, "We are your witnesses." And it was done.

So Boaz took Ruth as his wife and she conceived and they had a son. And the women of the town raised praises to God that Naomi had a grandson. And they praised God that she had a daughter-in-law who loved her and was better to her than seven sons. A daughter-in-law who stuck by her and brought her happiness in her old age. And Naomi took the child and laid him in her lap and cared for him as if he were her own flesh and blood. And they named him Obed. And in time Obed had a son and he was called Jesse. And in time Jesse had a son and he was called King David.

And Ruth, the Moab girl, was the great-grandmother of the greatest king Israel ever had.

Who was the hero here? Ruth? Naomi? Boaz? How about all three? They all were loyal and loving and dedicated to God and to each other. A good family in the family of God.

Now if you go to traditional history books, you will find history that is not recorded in the divine Scriptures. In these books you will find records that the Church of the Nativity in Bethlehem is built over a room that is said to be part of the ancestral home of David. This room was the very room where Ruth and Boaz slept and conceived the royal lineage. Also, it is said, 1,100 years later, this room had become a stable. And in this very room, Christ himself was born.

All part of God's glorious plan? I think so.

# ELIJAH

1 Kings 17 – 2 Kings 2

Elijah, Elisha, Elias. These are names that are easy to confuse so let's straighten them out right away. Elijah and Elisha were two different people but were very close friends. Elijah, when referred to nearly a millennium later in the New Testament, was often called Elias. So Elijah and Elias were the same person. We will call him Elijah, his Old Testament name, for the purpose and duration of our story.

Elijah was a prophet of God. He just pops up toward the end of the book of 1 Kings and I do mean pops up. No explanation of his beginnings or history. A simple mention that he was a Tishbite from Tishbe is all we have. Tishbe is never mentioned again anywhere in the Bible. It's as if he just appears and begins doing what he does, and after we look at what he does, his appearance is not all that unusual.

One day he appears standing beside King Ahab who was the worst king Israel ever had. He was evil. He was a heathen. He was no good through and through. Elijah, from out of nowhere, appears and says, "Ahab, as sure as my Lord God lives, there is not going to be rain in your kingdom for the next few years. Not until *I* say rain will there be even a dew in the early morning."

Now I've told you how mean and no good Ahab was, so it won't surprise you that the next voice Elijah heard was God telling him to get out of Ahab's sight and to do it quickly. King Ahab was not a man with a sense of humor and he didn't take bad news very well, so God told Elijah, "Get out of here and go down to the Kerith Ravine and you'll find a brook there to camp by. Hide there where you'll have water and I'll order the ravens of the air to feed you. They'll bring you bread and meat every morning and bread and meat every evening."

Elijah did just as God told him and he lived there by the brook and by the charity of the ravens until the brook dried up just like all the water in the area had, as he predicted it would. A victim of his own vision, he waited for further instructions from God and got them. "Go down to Zarephath. I've arranged for a widow in that town to feed you and care for you," God told him.

Sure enough, just as he was entering the gates of the city, he saw a woman gathering sticks from the dirt. He called to her, "Would you bring me a jar of water?" And as she started after it as he had requested, he added, "And while you're at it, bring me something to eat, too." Sort of like what a man lying on the sofa watching a football game might say.

The woman turned and looked at him and said, "I don't have anything to eat. I don't even have any bread. All I have is a handful of flour and a little cooking oil in a jug. I was gathering these sticks to make a fire to fix a final meal for my son and me. We're going to eat it and then we're going to die." The drought was taking its toll on everyone. They were starving to death and this was their last scrap of food.

Elijah said, "Don't be afraid. Just go and do what I asked of you. Make me a small cake of bread and bring it to me and then go and make the same for yourself and your son and I promise you'll have plenty leftover and will have plenty until this drought is over."

She did as she was instructed and everything Elijah had told her came true. This story was referred to by none other than Jesus years later in the Book of Luke. He talks about Elijah and the widow of Zarephath, a Gentile woman, just before he gets run out of his hometown. His homefolks didn't want to hear about a Gentile finding favor with God.

Days, weeks, months later, we don't really know how long, the son of this kind woman became seriously ill. He started getting worse and worse and finally just quit breathing altogether. The widow came running to Elijah. "Come quick, I think my son is dead." It certainly looked like he was and she somehow blamed Elijah for it. "You've come and caused my son's death because of my past sins, haven't you?" she yelled at him. She was frustrated and frightened and saying all those things we say when we're scared beyond all reason.

Elijah, in his wisdom simply said, "Give me your son" and took him in his arms and ran upstairs with him and lay him out on the bed and then stretched himself over top of him and prayed, "Lord, let this boy's soul come back into him."

He did this three times and after the third, the boy started to breathe. And Elijah picked him up and carried him downstairs and took him to his mother, alive and well. The widow of Zarephath said, "I know now that you're a man of God and that you speak the truth."

Elijah II

Three years passed and God told Elijah to go back and see King Ahab. He said, "Tell Ahab I'm ready to send some rain."

So faithful old Elijah headed back to the castle, but on his way he ran into Obadiah, King Ahab's right-hand man. The strange thing was that Obadiah was a God-fearing believer among the king's other pagan employees. Even the king's wife, Jezebel, was having every prophet of God killed that she could discover, so Obadiah was in dangerous company.

The king had called Obadiah in and sent him on a mission throughout Samaria to find any drop of water he could. He told him to look for springs and even green grass to feed the horses and mules. And it was while out on this assignment that Obadiah came upon Elijah and recognized him as the prophet of God and fell on his face on the ground at his feet.

They talked and Elijah told him to go and tell the king that he wanted to see him. Obadiah jerked his head back and said, "No way. Do you realize that Ahab has been searching for you for three years in every surrounding nation? And you want me to go and tell him I've found you and then when I get back here with him and can't find you, don't you realize I'll be a dead man? No way. Just leave me out of it."

Elijah promised him that he wouldn't run. He assured him that he would be there when he got back with Ahab, so Obadiah trusted him and went and found the king and brought him out for a meeting.

When they met face to face, because he had only seen him once three years before, Ahab said, "Are you the trouble-maker of Israel?"

Elijah said, "No. You're the troublemaker of Israel.

You're the one who has forsaken God. You're the reason for this horrible drought." And here we have to realize what a problem a drought was in this desolate desert. No rain, no water. No rain, no food growing. No rain, no livestock. The country was in complete turmoil and desperation. And why? This is where Elijah nailed the reason right in front of Ahab and laid it at his feet. He said, "You have been worshiping Baal."

And Baal was simply a gold statue, a god they prayed to and bowed down to. And the next words out of Elijah's mouth were about to prove for all generations who have the eyes to read and the heart to understand the difference between God and a god.

"I tell you what, Ahab. You bring all the people of Israel out here to Mount Carmel and also bring all the prophets of Baal, all 450 of them, and I'm going to challenge those prophets in front of the entire population."

Ahab went home and sent out word he wanted everyone, and he meant everyone, to come to the top of Mount Carmel outside the city. And when they got there, the people and the prophets of Baal and the king, Elijah presented his challenge. And here is the challenge and the story.

Elijah said, "I'm only one prophet and you're 450. Get two bulls and bring them here. Then choose the one you want. Then slaughter it and cut it into small pieces and lay the meat on the firewood but don't light the fire and I'll do the same thing with the other bull."

This was done. Elijah said, "Now the bulls are ready to cook. All we need is fire. So you call on the name of your god and I'll call on the name of my God and whoever answers with fire, is God. If your god answers, follow him. But if my God answers, you must follow Him."

The people liked this game. They all cheered and said what a good idea this was.

The prophets of Baal went first. From early morning till noon they prayed and chanted and cried and jumped and yelled for fire, but to no avail. No fire. "Answer us please, Baal," they begged. But Baal just couldn't seem to hear them.

At this point, Elijah showed a rare and sarcastic sense of humor. He began to taunt them. He said, "Shout louder. Maybe he can't hear you. Maybe he's busy or gone on a trip. Or maybe he's asleep. Holler louder. He'll hear you."

They yelled louder and cried with a passion and even pulled out their swords and slashed themselves in frustration until they were bloody. They kept this up until late into the evening, but nothing happened. Baal was not answering and now it was Elijah's turn.

He, this prophet of God, walked over to the bull they had prepared for him. And there it was, laid out on the altar, cut into small pieces atop dry firewood just waiting for the spark of a fire. He picked up 12 rocks, one for each of the 12 tribes of Israel, and built a small altar beside the sacrificial remains of the bull. Then he began to dig a large trench all the way around the bull and the altar and when he'd finished he told a few men to go and get him four barrels of water.

Water? Four barrels of precious, scarce water? But they did and when they came back with it he told them to pour the barrels on the bull and the wood and they soaked it there in the desert heat. And then Elijah said, "Do it again," and they brought four more barrels from God only knows where and poured them on the altar. And a third time.

Now 12 barrels of water are drenching the bull, the firewood, and filling the trench that encircles it. And only then did Elijah step back and caution the people to step back. And he raised his head to heaven or maybe he bowed it and said, "God, let them know that you are God."

Fire shot down from heaven and consumed the bull, the firewood, the altar and dried up every drop of water standing in the trench. And the people fell on their faces on the ground and shouted, "The Lord is God. The Lord is God."

Elijah had proven his point and won, but this was not the end of it. This is a great story in itself, but there is yet another end to come. He didn't just win and convert and ride off into the sunset. No, he took it up at least one more notch before he called it quits. He immediately said to the people, "Take all 450 of these prophets of Baal, and don't let any of them get away, and march them down the valley and . . . kill them!"

Elijah was a sore winner. He made his point and then he just kept on making it. All in the name of God. He turned to King Ahab, who had been watching all of this and said, "You better get something to eat and drink and then get out of here fast because the rain is coming." And while Ahab ate, Elijah climbed to the top of Mount Carmel.

He sat down and put his head between his knees and rested. And why not? He had done a pretty good day's work. He had called up a miraculous fire from God and had 450 men killed. He deserved a little rest and as he sat there he told his manservant to go look out toward the sea and to come back and tell him what he saw. He did and came back and reported that he saw nothing unusual at all.

"Go back and look again," Elijah commanded. And again the servant came back with nothing to report.

Seven times Elijah sent him to look toward the sea and

on the seventh time he came running back and said excitedly, "I just saw a little cloud coming up out of the sea and it was shaped like a man's hand."

Elijah said, "Go tell Ahab to get in his chariot and get out of here. The rain is coming!"

And as the black clouds rolled in and opened up, Ahab raced back to town in his chariot while Elijah, who had taken his coat off and tucked in his belt, ran . . . ahead of the chariot, back to town and shelter.

It is said the "power of the Lord came upon Elijah," this man who could call up fire from heaven, who could raise young boys from the dead, who could kill enemies by the hundreds, and who could outrun horses in the rain.

Elijah III

When King Ahab got home from his little excursion with Elijah, he told his wife, Jezebel, what all had happened. Now Jezebel was an evil woman and her name has lived down through the centuries as being synonymous with the image of a mean and conniving woman. She was big on Baal worshiping and would have anyone who wasn't put to death in a heartbeat. And it's needless to say that when she heard what a fool Elijah had made out of her husband and her god, she was furious.

She sent a message to Elijah that she was going to kill him. And not just a simple threat. Her words dripped in blood and determination. What she actually said was, "May the gods deal severely with me if by tomorrow at this time I don't have you as dead as every one of those prophets you killed." She was serious and Elijah knew she was serious. And he knew she was mean and he did what we might think is a strange thing for him to do. He ran.

A man who had just stood out there on the mountain and performed the miracle he performed and had just had 450 men killed, ran from this woman. But isn't that human? We all know a loud woman can do things to even the most resolute heart. And Jezebel did, because Elijah ran and hid in the desert.

He stopped to rest under a juniper and prayed that he would die. He was just fed up with his mission. He prayed, "Lord, take my life. I'm no better than my fathers before me." Poor ole Elijah was burned out.

He fell asleep and while he slept someone came and tapped him on the shoulder and woke him. It was an angel. And there on the ground beside him was a fire and hot bread and a jug of water. The angel told him to get up and eat and after he had done what he was told, he lay back down and went to sleep. Again the angel woke him and told him to eat some more because he was about to take off on a long journey and he'd need his strength.

He did what the angel commanded again and then got up and traveled for 40 days and 40 nights till he came to Mount Horeb, where he found a cave and went in and spent the night.

This time something woke him but it wasn't a tap on the shoulder. It was the voice of God. "What are you doing here, Elijah?"

"Well, God, I've done everything you wanted me to do and I'm the only one left and now they're trying to kill me."

God said, "Elijah, go out and stand on the mountain. The Lord is about to pass by."

But before Elijah could move, there was suddenly this terrible and powerful wind, a destructive tornado that just tore the mountain apart and shattered the rocks. But when it was over, Elijah realized that God was not in that wind.

And then the earth around him was shaken by a massive earthquake. But when that was over he knew that God was not in that either.

Then a horrible and raging fire that consumed every bush and tree in sight, but when that was over, Elijah knew God was not in the fire.

And when all of these powerful forces of nature, the wind, the earthquake, and the fire had subsided, he heard a small, gentle whisper and he knew that this was God. He learned that God doesn't always knock us over to get our attention. Sometimes He has to, but sometimes He just talks to us and calls our names in the quietest and most gentle way. And if we're always listening for it, we hear Him. And Elijah heard Him and walked to the adit of the cave and God talked to him and told him what he wanted him to do. Elijah listened and set out on his journey and in the course of his mission ran up on a young man named Elisha plowing the fields of his father. He stopped and took off his coat and put it on Elisha and told him to follow him and be his assistant. Elisha did and much after this becomes Elisha's story. But we'll visit with him another time. There's still a good deal more Elijah did with and without his assistant.

ELIJAH IV

Old Elijah disappears for a while to pop up again in what we might call The Case of the Stolen Vineyard. He's back with his old nemesis, King Ahab, and his lovely wife, Jezebel. It seems King Ahab had a neighbor named Naboth, who had a vineyard that butted up against the palace property that Ahab decided one day he wanted. He went to neighbor Naboth and said, "I want your vineyard. I've decided to tear it up and put a vegetable garden in it. I'll give you a better vineyard somewhere or I'll pay you whatever you think it's worth."

I'm sure this seemed like a fair deal in the arrogant, bully mind of King Ahab. He probably thought he had offered a real sweet deal and that coming from the king, no one would have the nerve to refuse him. But Naboth did. He said, "Thanks, but no thanks. My father left me that vineyard and it's very special to me and I want to keep it in the family."

Ahab, being the man he was, went home angry and sulked and lay on his bed and pouted and wouldn't eat. Jezebel, his wife, came in and saw him and said, "What's wrong with you?"

"I want Naboth's vineyard and he won't give it to me."

Jezebel, stronger and meaner than her royal husband, said, "Get up and get over it. I'll get you the vineyard." And she set her elaborate scheme into motion.

Jezebel wrote letters to certain elders and noblemen in the city and signed the king's name and used the king's seal so that they thought the letters were from the king himself. In the letter she told the leaders of the city to proclaim a holiday, a day of fasting that would gather all the people together. And in the midst of all this, hire two scoundrels, two criminals, and see that they were seated directly across from Naboth. And at the right time, have them bring charges against him and say that he blasphemed and cursed both God and the king and then take him out and stone him to death. Folks, this was a mean woman.

All of this was done just as she ordered. The letters went out, the day was proclaimed, the hired criminals were put in place, the charges were made, and the execution was carried out. And word was sent back to Jezebel that Naboth was dead. A triumphant Jezebel went in to her husband and said, "Ahab, you know that vineyard you wanted? Well, it's yours. Naboth is dead."

And Ahab got up and went down and walked around in his new vineyard.

Enter Elijah, the Tishbite, again. God came to him and said, "I want you to go back and see King Ahab one more time. Right now as we speak, he is standing in a vineyard in Samaria by his palace. I want you to say this to him. Tell him the Lord says, "You have killed a man and taken his property. Where the dogs licked up Naboth's blood, they will also lick up yours."

So Elijah once more heads out for the castle and finds the king standing in his newly acquired vineyard. Ahab sees him coming and greets him with, "So you have found me, my enemy."

"Yeah, I've found you and I'm mad."

And in the fear of paraphrasing, let me tell you exactly what Elijah said next to King Ahab. According to the King James Version of the Bible, Elijah said, and I quote, "Behold I will bring evil upon thee and will take away thy posterity and will cut off from Ahab him that pisseth against the wall and him that is shut up and left in Israel."

Now you may find this language a little unusual and not what you thought was in the Bible, but it is. This phrase, "him that pisseth against the wall," shows up in the Old Testament five different times and each time it means "male." Males as opposed to females, and I think that is explanatory enough. He is saying God is going to kill all the future males in Ahab's family and even all the male slaves.

Then he goes on to say, "The dogs will not only lick your blood, but will eat your descendants and concerning your wife, the dogs will eat her, too."

When Ahab heard all this, he tore at his clothes in agony and put on sackcloth, a cheap and humbling garment, and began to fast and repent. And when God saw him do all this, he said to Elijah, "I see how Ahab has humbled himself so I won't do these things to him while he's alive. I'll wait and bring these hardships on his son and his family after Ahab is dead."

So God let Ahab off the hook.

Three years later, Ahab was at war and he entered into a fierce battle. Even though he was heavily armored, an arrow found its place between sections of his breast protector and he was seriously wounded. The battle raged all day long and he was propped up in his chariot facing the enemy where he could watch the fight, blow by blow. And all day long blood ran from his wound onto the floor of the chariot and late that evening he died.

He was brought back to Samaria to be buried and his chariot was taken down to a pool where the harlots bathed to be cleaned up. And as it sat there to be washed and scrubbed, dogs came and licked at his blood that had run over the floorboard where he had stood all day long. And God's Word became the truth it had always been.

Eleven years after Ahab's death, during the rule of King Jehu, one of his main duties was to wipe out the house of Ahab. As soon as Jehu was anointed king, he headed for Jezreel, the home of Jezebel. She heard he was coming and like an old Hollywood vamp she dressed in her finest and put on her make-up, painted her eyes and combed her hair, and stood at an upstairs window and awaited his arrival.

When she saw him enter the gates, she yelled down, "Have you come in peace, you murderer?"

Jehu stopped and looked up and yelled back, "Who is on my side?"

At this very moment, three eunuchs who were her personal servants, and who must have hated her for years, came up behind her. When Jehu saw them he said, "Throw her down!"

And the three eunuchs grabbed her from behind and threw her out of the window. Her blood splattered all over the wall of the house and all over the horses and the horses spooked and trampled her underfoot.

Jehu, apparently touched by this gruesome scene, got off his horse, went inside, and got something to eat. While he was eating he said to his men, "Go take care of that cursed woman. Bury her. After all she was the wife of a king and the daughter of a king."

So the men went back out into the street to get Jezebel's body, but it was gone. All they found were her skull, her feet, and the palms of her hands. They came back in and told the king what they had found. And the good king said, "This is as the Lord predicted through Elijah, the prophet. The dogs will eat her flesh and she'll wind up as nothing but dung on the fields. There will be nothing left of her so that anyone can say, 'This was Jezebel.' "

And again God's Word became the truth it had always been.

ELIJAH V

But back to Elijah. After Ahab died, his and Jezebel's son, Ahaziah, became the eighth king of Israel. And Ahaziah did his earthly best to carry on the spiritual family tradition. He worshiped Baal and continued to find displeasure in God's eyes.

One day Ahaziah was coming out on the porch from an upstairs room of the palace in Samaria and slipped and fell through the lattice work and hurt himself pretty badly. The injury was so bad that he got worried if he would ever recover, so he sent messengers out to consult Baalzebub, an idol in the city of Ekron, to see if he would ever get well. Baalzebub was another form of the major idol Baal, and his name means "Lord of the Flies."

God, seeing all of this taking place, called on faithful ole Elijah again. He said, "Elijah, there are some men coming from King Ahaziah on their way to Ekron to ask a question of the idol Baalzebub. I want you to go meet them and I want you to say this to them: 'Is it because there is no God in Israel that you are going off to consult Baalzebub? Tell Ahaziah that this is what the Lord says, that he will never get out of the bed he is lying in but that he will die where he lays.' "

Elijah did as he was told and the messengers did as they were told, and when Ahaziah heard the message he said, "What kind of man was this that told you to come back here and tell me all this?"

The messengers said, "Well, he wore a camel hair garment and wore a leather belt around his waist."

And Ahaziah knew immediately from the description who it was. He knew him from the days of his father. He knew who dressed in those wild man clothes. He said, partly to himself, "It was Elijah, the Tishbite."

Ahaziah knew he had to meet with and deal with Elijah, so he sent out a captain and 50 men to bring him back to the palace. The troops went out in search of Elijah and found him sitting on top of a hill. The captain took leadership by

the nape of the neck and yelled up to him and said, "Man
of God, the king says come down here."

Elijah looked down on him and his small army of 50
and said, "If I be a man of God, let fire come down from
heaven and consume you and all your men."

And as if on cue, a fire shot down from heaven and
killed all 51 of them.

Undaunted, Ahaziah sent out another captain and another 50 men and they found Elijah, the prophet, sitting on
the same hill. The captain hollered up, "Man of God, the
king said for you to come down, here and now!"

Elijah looked down on this captain and his 50, just as
he had the ones before them, and said, "If I be a man of
God, let fire come down from heaven and consume you and
all your men."

And it won't surprise you that it did. All 51 of them.

And it also won't surprise you that Ahaziah sent out
another captain and another 50 soldiers on the exact, same
mission. But this captain handled a dangerous situation with
a little sensitivity. After marching out in search of Elijah
and after finding him, the captain fell on his knees in front
of the prophet and said, "Have respect for my life, please,
and my 50 men. Let us live."

And an angel of the Lord said to Elijah, "Don't be
afraid. Go with this captain to see the king."

So Elijah went back to the palace and stood before the
king and delivered in person the message God had originally sent. Elijah said to Ahaziah, "This is what the Lord
says: Is it because there is no God in Israel that you send
messengers to consult with Baalzebub? Because you have
done this you will never leave this bed you are lying on. You
will die right here."

And King Ahaziah died, just as God had said he would. And just as God had declared his father would. And just as God had said his mother would.

Later, Elijah and his assistant, Elisha, were walking down the road. Elijah turned and said, "The Lord is sending me to Bethel, so you stay here."

Elisha said, "No. I'm not going to leave you."

So they walked on to Bethel. When they got there, a group of prophets came out along the road to greet them and a few pulled Elisha aside and said, "Do you know the Lord is going to take your master, Elijah, from you today?"

Elisha said, "Yes, I know, but don't say anything about it."

After the prophets left, Elijah said again to his young partner, "The Lord is sending me to Jericho, so you stay here."

Elisha said, "No. I'm not going to leave you."

So they walked on to Jericho. When they got to Jericho, another group of prophets came out to greet them and a few edged up to Elisha and said, "Do you know the Lord is going to take your master from you today?"

Again, Elisha said, "Yes, I know, but don't say anything about it."

Elijah turned a third time to his man Elisha and said, "Stay here. The Lord is sending me to the Jordan."

But Elisha replied, "No. I'm not leaving you."

And 50 of the prophets walked behind them until they reached the Jordan River and stood back a distance and watched as the two men stopped on its bank. This was the same river that John the Baptist would baptize Jesus in nearly a thousand years later. And on the bank of this not-yet-historic river, Elijah took off his coat, rolled it up and struck the water. And the water parted just as Moses had parted the Red Sea. Water rolled up on both sides and he and Elisha walked across the river, to the other side, on dry ground.

Both of them knew what was coming. They knew God was about to come for Elijah right then and there. They could feel it in the wind. They could feel the imminence of God himself in all of the nature around them. One final time Elijah turned to his dear and loyal friend and had a last request. "Before he takes me up, tell me what I can do for you."

Elisha looked him sadly in the eye and said, "Let me inherit a double portion of your spirit."

Elijah said, "You have asked a hard thing. But I'll tell you what. If you see me when God takes me up, you'll get your wish. But if you don't see me when he takes me, you won't get your wish."

And while they were still walking along, talking to one another, a chariot of fire and horses of fire suddenly swept past them and came between them and separated them and then a great whirlwind took Elijah, the Tishbite, the prophet of God, to heaven.

Elisha looked up and saw it all and knew that the mantle had truly been passed to him. He reached down and picked up Elijah's coat and walked back and stood on the bank of the Jordan. He rolled the coat as he had seen Elijah do and struck the water as Elijah had and the water parted and gushed up on each side and he walked alone, back to the other side, on dry ground.

When he reached the other side, he found the 50 prophets from Jericho still waiting. When they saw him they bowed down because they could tell he had in him the spirit of Elijah. But these prophets were not quite as smart as we might have given them credit for being because they said to Elisha, "Where's your master? Did the Lord pick him up in that whirlwind we saw and set him down on top of the mountain? We'll all go look for him."

"No. Don't do that," Elisha said.

But they persisted. And they kept persisting until he was ashamed to keep saying no and he finally said, "Okay, go ahead and look for him."

Fifty men went out and searched for three days for the elusive Elijah and on returning told Elisha they couldn't find him anywhere.

And Elisha, still in shock over losing his friend and still in shock over seeing the powers of heaven as no man had ever seen them before, said, "Didn't I tell you not to go?"

And that you might think was the end of Elijah. But maybe not.

Elijah was one of only two men who ever lived that got to heaven without dying. The other was Enoch, father of Methuselah and great-grandfather of Noah. Someone is bound to try to tell you that Moses fits in this category, too, but it's not true. Moses died alone in the valley of Moab and God buried him, but to this day no one knows where his grave is.

Elijah was just swept up! Never died. What happened to him? Well, that's a little bit of a mystery in itself. The Old Testament tells us God will send Elijah back "before the coming of the great and dreadful day of the Lord." All through the New Testament this is echoed as well. In the New Testament he is often referred to as Elias, but don't let this throw you.

Just as he was a wild man dressed in camel hair and leather in the Old Testament and appeared suddenly and mysteriously without any history whatsoever and left the earth even more miraculously, John the Baptist shows up in the New Testament 900 years later, born miraculously, a wild man dressed in camel hair and leather living in the desert, eating locusts and wild honey.

John said he was here to make a way for someone greater. Was he Elijah reincarnated? Oops! That's a dirty word to most Christians. The Bible never uses the word but it writes all around it.

Jesus said of John the Baptist in Matthew 11:14, "And if you are willing to accept it, he is the Elijah who was to come."

Matthew 17:10–13 says "And the disciples asked him, 'Why then do they say that Elijah must come first?' Jesus replied, 'Elijah has already come but they didn't recognize him but have done everything to him they wished. In the same way I will suffer at their hands.' Then the disciples understood he was talking to them about John the Baptist."

In Luke 1:17, the angel Gabriel came to John the Baptist's father before John's birth and told him he was to have a son. Gabriel said, "And he will go on before the Lord in the spirit and power of Elijah."

Yet on the other hand, in John 1:21, when the priests were questioning John the Baptist as to who he was, he said, "I am not the Christ."

They asked, "Are you Elijah?"

He said, "I am not."

So who was he? Jesus leads us to think John was Elijah. Gabriel leads us to think the same. But John says no. The Bible never openly supports reincarnation and any Christian worth his weight in Scripture will scold you for even using the word. But then all of us Christians know we aren't worth our weight in Scripture anyway, so why not enjoy the minds God has given us and explore every possibility and nuance the Scriptures tease us with.

Matthew and Mark both tell us that some people thought they heard Jesus cry out for Elijah on the cross just before he gave up his last breath.

Who was Elijah? How many was he? Was he never born? We know he never died. Did he live again? Will he live again? One of the great and important characters of the Old and New (?) Testaments.

 # ESTHER

The Book of Esther

The story of Esther is a history all by itself. Her deed is still celebrated to this day by the Jewish community as the Feast of Purim. Falling in mid-March, gifts are given, holiday meals are served and the entire book, ten chapters, of Esther is read aloud in the synagogue. And if you want a really good biblical trivia question to stump your peers sometime, the Book of Esther provides half the answer: "What two books in the Bible never mention God?"

And the answer is, of course, Esther. Although it's all about God and His people and His hand at work. (The other book is the Song of Solomon.)

We open up, not on our title character, but on the royal family of Persia. It's about 460 years before Christ, and King Xerxes (zurk' seez) is on the throne. He has been for three years and now he's giving a banquet and a celebration for all his officials and noblemen. It's a seven-day feast in the palace garden, which is decorated in white and purple linen, silver and gold, and black marble. The wine is flowing freely and the king and his court are getting gloriously drunk.

Inside the palace, Queen Vashti is giving a party of her own for the women. The scene is set and the tale begins.

On the seventh day of the party, King Xerxes called his seven eunuchs in and said, "Go get the queen for me. She's a beautiful, beautiful woman and I want all these friends of mine to see her. And be sure to tell her to wear the royal crown. And be quick about it."

But when the seven eunuchs returned, they were alone and sadly told His Majesty that the queen refused to come. Maybe she just didn't want to be the center of his drunken party, or maybe she didn't want to be bossed around or maybe she just didn't want to be queen anymore.

If the latter was her thinking, she was successful because Xerxes didn't take lightly to her refusal. He called his council together and said, "My wife, the queen, has disobeyed me and according to the law, what can be done about it?"

They all scratched their heads and chins over it for a while until finally Memucan, one of the nobles, stepped up and said, "What she has done is wrong. But even worse, when what she has done reaches the common women, it will set a precedent and they will all be standing up to their husbands and saying if Vashti doesn't listen to the king, we don't have to listen to you. It could start a feminist movement we could never stop. Therefore let me suggest that we put out a decree signed by the king that says Vashti can never again be in the presence of Xerxes. Sort of a royal peace bond. Then to seal the deal, let the king take a new queen to replace Vashti. Find someone who is better than her and make a public example of her."

The king and all the king's men cheered the motion and a decree went out to all the land, in many different languages, and it read that every man should be the king of his own household.

In time, King Xerxes's cabinet came to him and said, "We have an idea how you can find a new queen. Let's put out the word in all the provinces that the search for a beautiful young virgin is underway and the ultimate prize will be that she will become the queen. We'll gather the beauty contestants, bring them here to the harem, and let Hegai, the eunuch in charge of the harem, give the beauty treatments and train them in the graces they will need and then whichever one pleases you will become your queen."

Could any man turn down such a suggestion? Not Xerxes.

In the capital city of Susa, there lived a Jewish man by the name of Mordecai. He had an orphaned first cousin named Esther whom he had reared since she was a little girl as if she were his own daughter. Esther, now a lovely young woman, is described in the Scriptures as being "fair and beautiful." So it was a natural order of things that she went to the king's house with the other beauties of the land to be handed over to Hegai, the queen-maker. It is a general assumption that participation was mandatory for those who qualified.

Hegai took an immediate liking to young Esther and gave her special care. He gave her the beauty treatments and special health food and even assigned seven maids to her and gave her the best room in the house.

Cousin Mordecai kept a close watch on Esther. He not only instructed her not to reveal her nationality, as Jews weren't real popular in Persia, but he walked back and forth in front of the courtyard of the harem all day long, every day, to keep abreast of how she was and how she was being treated.

Before a girl could be presented to the king, she had to complete 12 months of beauty treatments — 6 months with oils and 6 months with perfumes and cosmetics. When she was called, she could take anything with her she wanted. She would enter in the palace in the evening; spend the night, and the next morning, come back to the harem. She would not return to the king unless he was pleased with her and called her back by name.

When Esther's time came, she entered the palace with nothing except what Hegai, her mentor, suggested. And Hegai must have taught her well or maybe her natural charms and beauty prevailed because the king fell for her. Out of all the other contestants, he crowned Esther queen and gave her a great banquet and proclaimed a holiday in her honor and gave gifts to everyone. Vashti was out; Esther was in. And Mordecai still walked the gates out front and Esther still kept her secret as Mordecai had instructed. A Jewish princess was now queen of Persia.

Mordecai kept his vigil outside the gates and got to know some of the regulars. Two of them were the king's guards, officers who guarded the front entrance. Disgruntled, the two of them got loose-tongued and started bragging about how they were going to assassinate the king for reasons known only to them. Overhearing this, Mordecai went to Esther and told her, who in return got word to the king, who in return had the two officers hanged from the highest tree. Mordecai was now in solid with the king as he got credit for uncovering the entire plot.

Esther II

King Xerxes saw fit to promote a man in his cabinet of advisors, named Haman, to the highest position of all the noblemen. On the king's orders, every official and civilian alike knelt when Haman passed through the king's gate, but Mordecai, a mainstay at the gate, refused to bend his knee. When approached about it by some in the king's court and asked why he refused to bow to the newly promoted Haman, he said nothing and continued to show his disrespect by ignoring Haman when he walked by.

What Mordecai was not telling was that Haman's people, the Amalekites, were the oldest and bitterest foes of Israel and, being a Jew, Mordecai just could not bring himself to be subservient to this ancient enemy. So he remained silent and steadfast in his actions until finally Haman himself noticed what was taking place. He investigated it and found out that Mordecai was a Jew and this did not make him happy.

His only thought was how best to deal with it. He could have Mordecai killed but he wanted more. He wanted rid of the entire race. He wanted a way to wipe out not just the one man, but every Jew who lived in Persia.

So Prime Minister Haman and his staff sat down and "cast the pur" or "rolled the die" in our language. Or to make it plural, cast the purim or rolled the dice. And the roll came up 13 and 12 and their plan was afoot. They would carry out their terrorist attack, if they could get it by the king, on the 13th day of the 12th month. Now all that was left was to sell Xerxes on the idea and Haman was sure he could handle this.

"King Xerxes, your honor and majesty, there are certain people scattered out in your kingdom who are different from us. Their customs are foreign to our ways and they tend not to obey the king's laws. I feel it is not in the best interest of the king to tolerate these people and their arrogance. If it pleases the king, I suggest a decree be written and sent out to destroy these people. I believe in this matter so thoroughly that I will put up 10,000 talents of silver of my own money as bounty to the men who carry out this mission."

The king, with his trust fully in his newly appointed assistant, handed him his signet ring with which to seal the decree and said, "Keep your money, Haman. If this deed needs to be done, do it as you see fit."

So the royal secretaries were summoned and they wrote separate decrees in each language of each province to each governor and spelled out Haman's orders to kill all the Jews in the entire kingdom. Even women and children, young and old, were to be slaughtered on the 13th day of the 12th month, and the name of King Xerxes was signed to it and his signet ring was used to seal the wax.

Dispatches were sent out to every post by riders, very much like the early American Pony Express system. There were stations a day away from one another and deliveries of official importance traveled fast throughout the country. And once the couriers were launched, the king and Haman sat down and had a drink to a job well done.

As this tragic news leaked to the Jewish community throughout Persia, defenseless as they were, they openly cried and mourned for the destiny they saw coming. They put on sackcloth and lay in ashes as was their custom when grief-stricken or repentant. And Mordecai was no different from the masses. He tore at his clothes and wailed and wept at the gates louder than any others. He couldn't enter inside the gates because of his dress, as nothing as lowly as sackcloth was allowed in the king's courtyard.

Esther's maids came and told her about Mordecai and how he was dressed and how he was acting, so she sent clothes out to him so he could come in and see her. But Mordecai was having none of that. He refused the clothes and continued his ethnic custom.

Next, she sent out one of the eunuchs, Hatach, to talk to her cousin and find out exactly what was wrong with him as she was in the dark concerning anything about the decree.

Mordecai told him everything. All about Haman's plan to kill all the Jews, told him how much money he had offered from his own pocket to see it done, and gave him a copy of the decree to show to Esther. And as a final plea, he told Hatach to tell Esther to go to the king and beg him, if she had to, for mercy on behalf of her people.

Hatach took the message back to Queen Esther and in short time brought a message back. He said, "The queen says that for any man or woman to approach the king in the inner court without first being summoned by him is subject to the sentence of death. The only exception is if he sees you coming and extends his gold scepter to you. But this is risky, as you cannot know his reaction until you get there. And even as queen I can't go unless I'm called and he has not called for me for a month."

Mordecai sent his own message back to his cousin Esther. He told Hatach to say, "You must do something. Don't think just because you live in the king's house you will necessarily escape this massacre. If you remain silent and do nothing, deliverance will come from some place else I feel sure, but consider that maybe you have been put in this position at this particular time for this reason."

Old Mordecai must have hit the right nerve because Hatach was back in no time with this message from Esther: "Gather up all the Jews who are in the capital city of Susa and begin a fast for me. Don't eat or drink for three days and three nights. My maids and I will do the same here. When this is done, I'll go to the king even though I know it's against the law. And if I perish, I perish."

The Queen of Persia, the Heroine of Israel had spoken. No braver words are ever quoted in all the Bible. "And if I perish, I perish."

Mordecai carried out Esther's instructions and Esther and her maids began fasting in preparation of her duty to God and country.

On the third day, Esther dressed in her royal robes and stood in the hall of the palace in front of the king's door. King Xerxes was on his throne and when he saw her, he smiled and held up his scepter and Queen Esther walked the distance to her king and touched the tip of his scepter with her finger. All was well, so far.

"What is it, my queen? What do you want? Anything you ask for is yours up to half of my kingdom." That month and three days were in Esther's favor.

"I have come, if it pleases the king, to invite you and Haman to a banquet I am giving in your honor. Would you come?" Esther asked.

The king yelled to one of his servants, "Go get Haman. Tell him we're going to a party."

So the king and Haman went to Esther's party and as they were drinking, the king eyed his queen and asked again, "What exactly do you want? Just tell me and I'll give you up to half of my kingdom."

"Okay, this is what I want. I want to have a dinner again tomorrow for you and Haman. Then I'll answer your question."

The psychology of this postponement can only be assumed and realized as the story continues. It was Esther's plan to ingratiate Haman into the inner circle of the king and queen to the extent of irritation to the king and to also give credence to that old saw that "if you give a fool enough rope he will hang himself." Haman was the old fool and he went out immediately to achieve just that.

As he was leaving the palace in high spirits, he ran into Mordecai who again neither arose nor bowed as he passed. Rage and anger flew through him but he controlled himself and continued on his way home.

That night, sitting around with his wife and some of his friends, he got to boasting about how much money he had and how tight he was with the king. And he added, "Not only that, but today the queen had a luncheon and I was the only person invited besides the king. And tomorrow it's the same thing. Just me and the king and queen. But you know, even with all of that, there's still something that just rubs me raw and keeps me from enjoying my position, and that's that Jew, Mordecai, who sits at the gates and shows me no respect."

His wife, Zeresh, and his little group of friends said, "Tomorrow have a gallows built 75 feet high and ask the king personally to have Mordecai hanged on it. Then go to lunch with the king and forget about it and enjoy yourself."

"Hey, not a bad idea," Haman said.

And that night he ordered the gallows to be built.

ESTHER III

The king had trouble sleeping that night, so out of restlessness, he got up out of bed and called for a servant and demanded that someone read to him. And what he wanted read was his own biography; the history of his reign, his professional book of memories. And when the reader got to the part about the man at the gate named Mordecai who had saved the king's life by turning in two assassins, the king jumped up and said, "What did we ever do for that man? How did we honor him?"

"I don't think anything was ever done for him," the servant said.

It must have been early morning by this time because just as this conversation was taking place, the king heard someone walking in the outer court and said, "Who's out there?"

The servant looked and said, "It's Haman."

"Bring him in here," the king commanded.

And this is where the story comes together like an old 1930s screwball comedy of the silver screen. The plot of mistaken identities. Haman is there to persuade Xerxes to allow him to hang Mordecai, the rebel Jew, and Xerxes is calling Haman in to help him make a decision on how to *honor* Mordecai, the king's hero.

The servant goes and gets Haman and brings him in to the king. "Haman, what special thing should be done for a man the king wishes to honor?" Xerxes asked, seriously looking for suggestions.

Wow, Haman thought to himself. *He's getting ready to honor me! And he's even letting me pick the way I would like to be honored. Okay, I'll play along with his game.*

"Your majesty, for a man the king wishes to honor, I suggest you have them bring a royal robe the king has worn and a horse the king has ridden, one with a crest placed on his head. And then put the robe on this man you would like to honor and seat him on the horse and ride him through the city streets and proclaim to everyone 'This is what is done for a man the king wishes to honor.'"

Haman was pleased and smug. He had planned his own honor and was ready to feign surprise when the king announced, "It's you, Haman. It's you!"

But the next words out of the king's mouth were, "Then go get that robe and go get that horse and go get Mordecai the Jew and ride him through the streets and tell everyone that this is what is done for the man the king wishes to honor."

And Haman, broken and dejected, did as he was ordered. The man he had planned to kill would be the man to whom he would have to pay homage in front of the entire city. He went home after doing his duty of the king and covered his head in grief and whined to his wife and friends about his day and what he had been forced to do. And even while he was complaining, eunuchs came to his house and hurried him away and escorted him to Esther's banquet.

The king and Haman sat down to dine with the queen, and as they were drinking their wine, the king asked again as he had the day before, "What do you want, Esther? You can have anything you ask for up to half of my kingdom."

Esther took her chance, "O king, I feel I have found favor with you and here is my request. Grant me life and grant my people life for they have been sold for destruction and slaughter."

"And who is the man who dared do such a thing?" the king demanded.

"The evil Haman, your enemy," answered his queen.

And at this moment both Haman and the king put two and two together and realized that Esther was Jewish and that she was speaking of the decrees that Haman had authored, and by his hand had ordered the slaughter of all the Jews in Persia. Haman was terrified and the king was in a rage.

Xerxes stormed out into the palace garden leaving his

wine untouched on the table while Haman, ever the coward, stayed behind to beg the queen for his life. He knew his fate was fixed with the king and that his only hope was the mercy of Esther.

But the king was having his own struggle in the garden. Wild thoughts were surely running through his head. "My wife is Jewish? I had no idea. Haman is my enemy? He must be. He deceived me if he knew my wife was Jewish and talked me into wiping out her people. But maybe he didn't know. Whom do I believe? Who's the most important to me? Who's the most important to my kingdom? How did a simple little party turn into this?"

And as if things weren't in enough turmoil, when the king came back in from the garden he found Haman falling on top of Esther who was lying on the couch. Maybe she was lying there out of exasperation and maybe he was merely bending over her while pleading with her, but that's not the way Xerxes saw it. Xerxes said, "Are you trying to take advantage of my wife with me in the house?"

Haman's fate was surely sealed now.

Harbona, one of the eunuchs who had been watching this scene unfold spoke up to the king, "Haman had a gallows 75 feet high built beside his house. He was going to hang Mordecai on it."

The king shouted, "Hang *him* on it!"

And they did. They hanged Haman on the gallows he had built for Mordecai.

Esther IV

That same day, Xerxes turned everything Haman owned over to Esther. Esther, in return for this trust, came clean with the king. She brought Mordecai into the palace and told Xerxes who he was and how they were related and that they were both Jewish. The king took off his signet ring, the one he had taken off Haman before his walk to the gallows, and presented it to Mordecai. Esther signed over her newly acquired wealth to Mordecai. And all was well in the palace, but not in Esther's heart.

She fell at the king's feet and cried and begged, "Please put an end to this evil plan that Haman has put into motion. This plan to kill all the Jews in the kingdom."

King Xerxes raised his gold scepter as a sign for Esther to stand and speak.

"If you find favor with me, let a new order be written that cancels the old one that Haman sent out because I can't stand to see my family and all my people destroyed."

King Xerxes, the man on the spot, looked seriously at Esther and Mordecai and said, "I have hanged Haman and given his estate to Esther because he was going to attack the Jews. But to overturn an order from the king that has been signed and sealed by the king is impossible. However, we can write a new decree to the Jews that will give them the authority to defend themselves. Mordecai, you and Esther write something up however you want to say it, and we'll get it out immediately."

So again the royal secretaries were summoned and Mordecai, the new prime minister, dictated his message to all the Jews in Persia, granting them the right to assemble, arm and protect themselves, annihilate any national force that might attack them and do harm to their women and children, and to plunder the property of the enemy. The day designated for all of this to happen was the 13th day of the 12th month, the very day the first decree had ordered the original attack.

The dispatchers and riders were again put into motion and the "Pony Express" ride began. The couriers raced throughout the kingdom on mules and camels and royal horses. The decree went to every one of the 127 provinces and to every ruling governor, and the Jewish nation within a nation, had their mandate and their orders.

Mordecai, the gate sitter, walked out of the king's palace in a blue and white robe with purple linen, wearing a gold crown on his head. And every Jew cheered, both there and in every province. There were feasts and celebrations and many who weren't Jews, became Jews out of fear.

The king was no longer in charge of the castle. The queen and her family reigned. Long live the queen.

The 13th day of the 12th month was a day of reckoning. The army under the first decree attacked the Jews under the second decree. The army was scared and the Jews were angry, and their passion and determination overcame their enemy. And it didn't hurt any that their man was in power back at the palace. Mordecai was getting more prominent and more powerful every day. His reputation was spreading quickly and everyone trembled at the mention of his name.

The Jews won the war easily. They laid the enemy flat and did what they pleased to anyone who opposed or hated them. They rounded up the ten sons of Haman and killed them and then overtook the citadel, the fort, in the capital city and killed 500. The one order they didn't follow was the permission to plunder. They touched nothing.

When the king received this report, he went to Esther and told her, "They've killed Haman's sons, killed half a thousand at the citadel, and I can only imagine what damage they've done in the other provinces. What should we do? It's your decision. What should we do?"

Esther, still playing the king like a harp, said sweetly, "If it pleases the king, let the Jews continue as they are for one more day yet and let Haman's sons be hanged on the gallows."

So it was done. On the 14th day of the 12th month, the Jews in Susa hanged the bodies of Haman's sons and killed 300 more men.

Down in the provinces, the Jews killed 75,000 on the 13th, and on the 14th, they rested. They needed it.

Now the Jews in Susa fought on the 13th and the 14th and didn't rest until the 15th. This is an important fact. The fighting ended a day sooner out in the surrounding country than it did in the city. And that is why rural and village Jews celebrated this date on the 14th and the city-dwelling Jews, those living in walled cities, celebrated it on the 15th. Today, only Jerusalem celebrates the 15th. And the celebration is called Purim.

Why Purim? Because of the purim, or the dice, that were rolled to originally determine the day of the attack. To this day, Purim is a holiday celebrated by the Jewish community, usually in the month of March, by current calendars. The Megilla, another name for the Book of Esther, is read in its entirety in synagogue and whenever Haman's name is mentioned, the people use noisemakers and stomp their feet and clack rocks together; anything to *erase* Haman's evil name.

So at the end of our story, Mordecai is a powerhouse in Persia. He's running things his way and his people are in charge and he's a major folk hero. King Xerxes, in some Scriptures called King Ahasuerus, was still on the throne and seemed rather adept at letting good people do their jobs without interfering. And Esther, Queen Esther, daughter of

Abihail, first cousin of Mordecai, wife of Xerxes, and saver of the Persian Jews, was still the reigning queen.

Hero or outlaw? This is an easy one. Sure, she deceived her husband by hiding her heritage from him. She didn't lie to him. She just didn't tell him anything. Who of us are not guilty of sins of omission?

Whatever she lacked in that moment of truth telling, she certainly made up for with courage. She approached the king with her life at stake. She schemed her way through two banquets to trap Haman. And she petitioned the king for one more day of battle for her people. If that doesn't spell hero, or shall we say heroine, what does?

No braver words were ever spoken, "And if I perish, I perish."

JOHN THE BAPTIST

Matthew, Mark, Luke, and John

There was a priest in Judea named Zechariah. He and his wife, Elizabeth, were both very religious and up-right people. Elizabeth had resigned herself to the fact that she could never have children a long time ago, and now that she and her husband were old, the thought never crossed her mind.

One day Zechariah was in the temple alone burning incense, as was his duty, when an angel suddenly appeared, standing beside the altar. This was pretty rough on an old man's heart and he was honestly petrified by the sight. (Have you ever been in a church all alone, even in broad daylight? It's a lonesome, spooky feeling.) Then, like Zechariah needed more reason for his heart to stop, the angel spoke to him. And you can imagine how that affected him. The angel said, "Don't be afraid, Zechariah. I'm just here to tell you that you and Elizabeth are going to have a son. And he is going to be something! People are going to celebrate when he's born and he's going to be very special in God's eyes. But take note, Zechariah. Your son can never drink wine, as he will be filled with the Holy Spirit from the moment he is born. (John also was a Nazarite as Samson was.) He'll bring a lot of people back to God in his life span. His mission will be to go ahead of the Lord, in the name of Elijah (remember later that I said this), and he will prepare the people for Him. And, oh yeah, you are to name him John."

Well, Zechariah finally found his voice and was able to croak out his doubts and fears. He said, "How can I be sure of this? I mean, I'm an old man and my wife is an old woman and you pop in here and tell me we're going to have a baby."

The angel said, "My name is Gabriel and I have been sent here to give you this good news, but because you didn't believe me, I'm going to strike you dumb right now and you won't be able to speak a word until all of this is over."

When Zechariah came out of the temple, the streets were full of people waiting to go inside because by custom they couldn't enter until he had readied it for them. They were waiting patiently but certainly wondering what had kept him so long in there. I'm sure they were wondering just how long it takes an old priest to light a little incense. They had no idea he was in there talking to angels and they didn't hear it from him because when he came out they all talked to him but try as he may, he couldn't talk back to them. He kept trying to make signs to tell them what had happened but they couldn't understand. They knew he had seen some kind of vision in there but they couldn't make out what.

He went home that night in silence and that same night Elizabeth conceived. And Elizabeth knew. She knew this had come from God.

Six months went by. And now we switch over to a little town down the road and in sight of the village where

Zechariah and Elizabeth lived. And again we run up on this same angel, Gabriel, and this time he appears to a woman. The woman's name is Mary and he tells her that she, too, is going to have a baby in a miraculous way. In telling her, he says, "You know your cousin Elizabeth, over in the Judean hills? Well, she's going to have a baby, too. She was thought to be barren and is definitely past her child-bearing years, but she's now in her sixth month because nothing is impossible with God."

So Mary took off not long after this to visit her cousin Elizabeth, over in the Judean hills. And when Mary walked in the house and greeted her, Elizabeth felt the baby leap in her womb. And it's said that Elizabeth was filled with the Holy Spirit. And she was also very impressed and overcome with the fact that cousin Mary had decided to come visit her. She asked, "Why am I favored with a visit from the mother of my Lord?"

So you see Elizabeth was one of the first believers in Christ. Mary believed what was happening to her from the very first and now Elizabeth believed even before He was born.

And six months before Jesus was born, we see John born. Thus, John and Jesus were cousins (second or third? we don't know) with John a half a year older.

On the day John was born, the people were all celebrating and rejoicing just like the angel had predicted. But mainly they were rejoicing because the elderly wife of the old priest had just had her first baby and they were all so happy for her. On the eighth day after birth, as was the Jewish custom, they all came to see him circumcised and witness him being named. The officials of the temple were about to name him after his father, when Elizabeth spoke up right in the middle of the ceremony and stopped them. Elizabeth spoke up because she was the only one in the family who could. Remember poor old Zechariah couldn't say a word and hadn't for over nine months.

Elizabeth said, "No. We are not naming him after his father. His name is to be John."

And the officials looked at this irrational woman and said, "But there is no John in any of your families. We'll name him Zechariah after his father."

And they turned to Zechariah and made signs to him asking for his approval and permission to continue. But Zechariah waved his hands and frantically signaled for someone to bring him a tablet to write on. They brought him one and he wrote, "His name is John."

At this very second his mouth came open and his tongue was loose and he could talk. And he began praising God. Not questioning the God who had taken his speech, but praising the God who had given it back to him. And all the people standing around watching were in awe but didn't quite know what was going on. They said to each other, "What is this child going to be, because surely the Lord's hand is with him." They knew something special was happening, they just didn't know what.

And we're told, "The child grew and became strong in spirit and lived in the desert until he appeared publicly to Israel."

Jesus and John. Born within six months of each other and grew up in towns in sight of each other. Maybe they played together as children or at least visited one another. We don't know. We don't know what they may have talked about if they did visit, but it must have been one heavenly conversation.

JOHN THE BAPTIST II

John was now a grown man. The year was around A.D. 26 and he and Jesus were both about 30 years old. John was living in the desert and was somewhat of a wild man. He was wearing rough outdoorsy clothes made from camel's hair, and I don't mean a camel's hair sweater here. He was wearing camel hide with a leather belt around his waist and he lived off the land. He ate a diet of locusts and wild honey and that is a diet by anyone's standard. I would picture him from this description as very, very thin, wiry, dirty, with long unkempt hair. I think it safe to say, feral looking. But a very godly man. That old adage about a book and its cover would apply to, if not define, John.

He was preaching to the people who came to him and they were coming to him in droves. They wanted to hear and be baptized. Seven hundred and fifty years earlier, in the Old Testament, Isaiah predicted the activities of John. He wrote of "a voice of one calling in the desert and preparing a way for the Lord." And it all came true.

But this voice was not always soothing and peaceful. John's message was hard and coarse and to the point. He preached, "Repent for the kingdom of heaven is at hand." He preached terror and fear and opened his sermons with this greeting, "You bunch of snakes, listen to me. Just because you're Jewish" (which he was, too), "don't come out here thinking you're going to get special privileges. Just because you can trace your ancestry back to Abraham, don't think that's going to give you a special place in heaven. No, this salvation is for everybody. So get used to it."

The crowds looked at him in bewilderment and said, "Wh . . . Wh . . . What do you mean? What do we have to do?"

And this is where he laid it on them good. Where he laid it on us good. This is what he threw back to the crowd and their question while looking them directly in the eye and in the heart. He said, "You got two coats? Give one to somebody who doesn't have a coat. You got food? Give some to somebody who has no food at all."

The tax collectors and the soldiers all asked, "What should *we* do?"

John said, "You don't have to give up your work to find salvation. Just take pride in your work and in your job and do it the best you can. As fair as you can. Be honest and don't cheat anyone. There is no better way you can serve than in your daily job. Do it and do it well and do it in God's name."

And all the people listened to him and marveled at him and said, "Are you the Messiah? The one we have been waiting for?"

John said, "No, I am not the Christ."

"Then who are you? Are you Elijah?"

"I am not."

"Are you the prophet?"

"No."

"Well, tell us something. Give us something to take back. Who are you?"

"I am the voice of one calling in the wilderness, making a way for the Lord. I baptize with water but He baptizes with the Holy Spirit. He comes after me and I am not even worthy to carry His sandals."

So his name was John and he baptized people. Thus, John "the Baptist." And "to baptize" means to cleanse, purify, wash away. To repent of sins and prepare for a cleaner and more spiritual life. But we know what comes next in this story. Jesus is about to show up and be baptized by this wild man. And why? Certainly Jesus doesn't need to be baptized. And certainly not by a mortal man so much lesser than He. What is going on here?

Scholars have bounced this one around for years. Maybe, they say, Jesus got baptized to satisfy His mother. He performed his first miracle at the Cana wedding, when He turned the water into wine, to satisfy His mother. Or maybe He got baptized to set a good example for His brothers. He definitely had little brothers. Maybe He did it to show approval of his cousin John. Or maybe to publicly announce the beginning of his ministry. Or maybe so God could publicly anoint Him. One of these, certainly, is the reason and maybe all of them, because he did not have the need you and I have to be baptized.

The Gospel According to the Hebrews is a history book that is not included in the New Testament for reasons unknown to me, but in this book is written the following Scripture:

> The mother of the Lord and his brothers said to him, "John the Baptist baptizes for the remission of sins. Let us go and be baptized by him." But Jesus said to them, "What sin have I committed that I should go and be baptized by him?"

So there you go. Maybe he *did* do it to satisfy his mother. But for whatever reason, he came to the Jordan River, face to face with cousin John. And when he stood eye to eye with him, John said, "No. I can't baptize you. You should be baptizing me."

But Jesus stepped into the water and John did the

honors. And as Jesus was coming up out of the water, out of the river, heaven opened up and the Spirit of God came down from heaven in the form of a dove and sat on Jesus' shoulder. Then a voice from heaven was heard and it said, "This is my son, whom I love, and with whom I am well pleased."

So maybe He didn't do it for His mother after all. Maybe he did it for His Father.

John The Baptist III

So now we have Jesus ready for His ministry and John deep into his. John and his disciples are out baptizing and Jesus and His disciples are out baptizing. Some of John's followers didn't take to the competition too well. They got defensive and argued among themselves and finally went to John, himself, and said, "You know that man that was in the Jordan with you and you testified about? Now He's out baptizing, too, and all kinds of people are going to Him instead of us." They saw it as a contest and didn't like losing customers to the opposition.

So John had to calm them down. He said, "That's a whole other thing He's doing. He's doing something I can't do and I'm happy and you should be, too. He's like the bridegroom and I'm like a friend of the bridegroom. The best man. The shoshben." In the Jewish faith that is what the best man is called. The shoshben. He is in charge of the wedding; at the bridegroom's beck and call. His job is to see that it all comes off all right. He doesn't begrudge the groom and the bride the glory of the day. He's just there to serve and assist.

Yet even with Jesus and His disciples in full swing, it seemed that John and his band were getting hotter by the minute. His popularity was spreading and everyone was talking about "The Baptizer" who lived in the desert and dressed in animal skins and seemed to know God in a personal way. Even the sitting king got wind of this wild man's mission and took heed of the things he was saying.

This sitting king was Herod Antipas, son of King Herod who had had all the babies killed when Jesus was born. Old King Herod was terror on a stick. He not only killed other people's babies, he killed his own. He had at least three of his own sons killed for various and sundry reasons. There was even a joke going around the Jewish community then that went, "It is safer to be Herod's pig than Herod's son." They didn't eat pork so I'm sure this joke was way too true.

Anyway, by this time Herod Antipas was king. And one day he went to visit his half-brother, Phillip, who lived in Rome, and while he was there he fell in love with Phillip's wife, Herodias. Now follow me closely on this. Herodias was not only Herod Antipas's half-brother's wife, she was also the daughter of another half-brother of Antipas's which would make her Antipas's niece. So he falls in love with his sister-in-law who is also his niece and persuades her to go back to Jerusalem with him and marry him. She does and brings her daughter with her who is not only Antipas's great niece but now is also his stepdaughter.

Now if this sounds like a comedy routine, it sort of is. But John the Baptist, out there preaching fire and brimstone, saw no humor in it. He felt national leaders should show a good example and a little restraint when it came to sexual fidelity and he went to Herod Antipas and told him so.

Made ole Antipas mad. So mad, he had John arrested. He wanted to kill him but he was afraid to because John was so popular and had such an influence over the people.

You see, Herod Antipas was a politician of the first order and didn't want to lose favor with the public. He also didn't want to lose favor with his dear wife/sister-in-law/niece because the more stink John made about their relationship, the more embarrassed she got and the more pressure she put on her husband/brother-in-law/uncle to do something to shut up "that wild, crazy baptizer." So he just threw him in prison to get him out of his face for a while.

So now John is sitting in prison and Jesus is out preaching. And a very strange and unexpected thing happens. John, from prison, sends two of his disciples out to find Jesus and to ask Him a question. And that question is, "Are you the one who was to come or should we expect someone else?"

This is very shocking. Could John be doubting who Jesus really was?

He had preached that Jesus was the Messiah, the Savior, and he had even baptized Him. And hadn't he known Him all his life? Was he not even kin to Him? But now, in prison, he was having second thoughts. Maybe. We're not sure. Maybe prison life is getting to him.

Scholars speculate that maybe he was getting impatient and felt that Jesus would or should have done something miraculous by now and that he should be free from prison. Or maybe he had no doubts at all. Maybe he was doing it for the sake of his disciples who were getting fidgety and doubtful. So he said, "Go out and find Jesus and ask Him for yourself who He is." Or maybe he was just looking for confirmation and plain old human reassurance.

For whatever reason, Jesus understood. He told John's disciples, "Go back and tell John what you've seen and heard out here. Tell him the blind see, the lame walk, the deaf hear, leprosy is cured, and the dead are raised from the grave."

They left with that message and after they did, Jesus turned and talked to the crowd about John. He said, "What did you go in the desert to see? A weak man, a man dressed in fine clothes or a prophet? I tell you, you saw more than a prophet. This is the one. John is the one they wrote about hundreds of years ago [in the Old Testament] when they wrote 'I will send one ahead of you who will prepare the way for you.'"

And then Jesus said a very reassuring thing to us all. He said, "I tell you, among those born of women, there is no one greater than John, yet the one who is least in the kingdom of heaven is greater than he." (Read that last sentence again and let it sink in if it will and everything else you ever read will pale in comparison).

Jesus went on to say, "John came neither eating bread nor drinking wine" (a Nazarite eating locusts and honey), "living in the desert wearing camel hair coats and for all his ascetic ways you called him a madman, a wild man. Then I came and I ate and drank and mixed with poor and ungainly people and you called me a glutton and a drunkard and low class. What do you want? You find fault in everyone if you look for it. But I tell you, wisdom will prove itself in the end."

Jesus showed his final and complete approval of John. He was not offended if he thought John had doubted him. He was not offended by the questions of the disciples. But he was offended by the judgments of the people. He had a mysterious way of turning a question into a scolding answer and anger into a loving gesture. His message was simple but he, many times, was very complex.

John testified at one time that he knew this was the Son of God. Then in prison he appeared to need reassuring. Why?

How about just to show us we're not lost when we need our faith bolstered from time to time? We're all human, just like John.

Now let's get back to Herod Antipas. He's in his castle and John is in his prison for speaking out against his incestuous marriage and his multi-related wife. It's Antipas's birthday and he's having one heck of a party. He's in the banquet room with all of his high officials and military commanders and they are partying down big time. The wine is flowing, the buffet tables are spilling over, the music is blaring and the beautiful girls are flitting about to the delight of every guest, when all of a sudden amid the dancing girls, out comes Salome dancing a dance of her own. Now this was Antipas's step-daughter/great niece and she was an apparent beauty. She began doing this provocative little dance and Herod Antipas and all his cronies were getting pretty entertained by it all, as they were also a little high on the fruit of the vine. When she finished her slithering dance, H.A., playing big man in front of his friends, called her over and said where everyone could hear, "You have pleased me greatly, Salome. Ask me for anything and I'll give it to you. Anything you want, I'll give it to you, up to half of my kingdom."

Does this sound like a half-drunk old man infatuated with a pretty young face or what? And it certainly was not the last time an old fool would make a promise to a young sweetie, but one lesson to be learned here is to never do it in front of witnesses. Too late for old H.A. Salome looked at him and he knew immediately she didn't brush it off as a joke because her first reaction was to go and talk the offer over with her mother. She said, "Mother, my daddy (or uncle H.A., I don't know which she called him) has offered me anything I want because he liked my dancing. Up to half of the kingdom. What should I ask for?"

Now we have a mother and daughter with their heads together with a promise of anything they want. Herod was in deep water and didn't even know it. But Herodias and her evil and deceitful ways, fool us right here. She doesn't ask for a new dishwasher or a larger chariot or even to have half the kingdom put over in her name. No, she asks for something that will give her great personal pleasure and relief. She said, "Tell him you want the head of John the Baptist."

So she did. To please her mother, who wanted to quiet John for good from ever speaking out against her in public again, Salome walked back in the banquet room and in front of all the dignitaries and friends of the throne, she said, "I want the head of John the Baptist on a platter and I want it now."

Herod Antipas turned white. He couldn't move. And he couldn't refuse. Not here. Not now. Not in front of all these people who had heard the offer made. He really didn't want to kill John because of his popularity but he was on the spot. His wife was probably peeking through the curtains, laughing at him.

So Herodias had her way. The king sent immediately for an executioner and had John beheaded and his head brought into the party on a platter and presented to Salome. Salome took the platter and presented it to her mother. And John's disciples took his body and laid it in a tomb.

And that was the end of John the Baptist's life. But not the end of his mystery.

He was born miraculously to elderly parents. His conception and birth were pre-announced by an angel. He baptized the Lord himself. He was beheaded as a whim at a birthday party. He did not live a normal life. And the question was always with him as to who he really was. The question is always with us as to who he really was. There was more mystery to John even after he died. And still a mystery today.

Even though that was the end of his life, it was not the end of his story. There are other mentions of him in the gospels and one is shrouded and caked with ambiguity. We won't solve it here, as scholars, commentators, and masters of the Scriptures through the ages have shied away from it and won't touch it.

But here it is for you to ponder and figure out for yourself. Here is one of the last significant mentions of John in the Bible.

Jesus had just told His disciples that He was going to die. Then He retreated up onto the mountain and He took Peter and James and James's brother, John, with Him. And this was what has come to be known as the Transfiguration. Jesus transfigured, changed, into a spirit while standing up there and these three disciples watched Him. They said later that His face shone like the sun and His clothes became white as light. And if that wasn't enough to scare their smocks off of them, they said Moses, who had been dead for 1,300 years and Elijah, who had been dead for 900 years, appeared standing along beside Jesus. And the three of them, Moses, Elijah, and Jesus just stood there talking to one another. And then to top that off, there was suddenly the voice of God saying, "This is my Son in whom I am well pleased. Listen to Him!"

This is when Peter and James and John hit the dirt and covered their heads. And when Jesus said, "Get up. Don't be afraid," they got up and looked around and no one was there but Jesus.

After this they all walked down the mountain together, Jesus and the three disciples, and they were silent until Jesus spoke first. "Don't tell anyone what you have just seen up here until I have been raised from the dead."

Well, trying to absorb all this and having little time to get it right in their minds, they took this opportunity to start asking questions. One of them was still in shock over seeing Elijah, an Old Testament prophet. He had read about him all his life but now he had just seen him. So he asked, "Lord it says in the Scriptures that Elijah would come first, before you came. But yet he didn't, did he?"

Jesus said, "Elijah has come but they didn't recognize him and they killed him."

And the next verse reads, and I quote: "Then the disciples understood that he spake unto them of John the Baptist."

So who was John the Baptist? Jesus' second or third cousin? The Waymaker? Elijah reincarnated? That's a dirty word in our religion. But what else is to be made of this Scripture? Maybe only one person was ever reincarnated and it was John. Few people will offer an answer on this one. The decision is yours.

Hero or outlaw? He lived like a hero and died like an outlaw. He was executed in prison like a common criminal but lived a pure life in pursuit of his heavenly mission from the day he was born. Doing his job. Doing the Lord's work. Baptizing in the name of the Father and the Son and the Holy Ghost.